LET'S TALK ABOUT

RACE AND PRIESTHOOD

OTHER BOOKS IN THE

LET'S TALK ABOUT SERIES

Let's Talk about Polygamy

Let's Talk about Religion and Mental Health

Let's Talk about the Book of Abraham

Let's Talk about the Law of Consecration

Let's Talk about Faith and Intellect

Let's Talk about the Translation of the Book of Mormon

Let's Talk about Temples and Ritual

For more information on the other books
in the Let's Talk About series,
visit DesBook.com/LetsTalk.

LET'S TALK ABOUT

RACE AND PRIESTHOOD

W. PAUL REEVE

SALT LAKE CITY, UTAH

For Darius

© 2023 W. Paul Reeve

All rights reserved. No part of this book may be reproduced in any form or by any means without permission in writing from the publisher, Deseret Book Company, at permissions@deseretbook.com. This work is not an official publication of The Church of Jesus Christ of Latter-day Saints. The views expressed herein are the responsibility of the author and do not necessarily represent the position of the Church or of Deseret Book Company.

Deseret Book is a registered trademark of Deseret Book Company.

Visit us at deseretbook.com

Library of Congress Cataloging-in-Publication Data
(CIP data on file)
978-1-63993-119-4

Printed in the United States of America
PubLitho, Draper, UT

10 9 8 7 6 5 4 3 2 1

CONTENTS

Foreword by Darius A. Gray vii

Introduction 1

PHASE ONE:
UNIVERSAL PRIESTHOOD AND TEMPLES

1. Black Converts in the U.S. North 11

2. Black Converts in the U.S. South 18

3. Race Relations in Jackson County, Missouri . . . 24

4. Outsiders View the Latter-day Saints Racially . . . 31

5. Latter-day Saints and Slavery in the 1830s and '40s 34

6. Universalism at Nauvoo 41

7. Race at Winter Quarters 44

8. Old Testament Curses and the Book of Abraham 47

PHASE TWO:
SEGREGATED PRIESTHOOD AND TEMPLES

9. Latter-day Saints and the Fear of Race Mixing . . 57

10. Brigham Young Openly Articulates a Racial Restriction 62

11. Orson Pratt and a Premortal Explanation 70

CONTENTS

12. The Priesthood and Temple Restrictions in Practice 75

13. A One-Drop Policy 79

14. The Restrictions Harden in Place 85

15. A Lack of Consensus for Change 88

16. Racial Restrictions and the International Church 93

PHASE THREE:
A RETURN TO RACIAL INCLUSIVITY

17. The 1978 Revelation 103

18. Post-Revelation Justifications 110

19. Agency and the Gospel Plan 120

20. Prophetic Leadership 125

21. Jesus Christ Is Mighty to Save 127

22. A Path Forward 131

Further Reading 135

Acknowledgments 137

Notes 139

Index 157

FOREWORD

1993, Wybark, Oklahoma

The little cemetery both looked and felt completely different from the first time I had stood there. It had been two years since the family reunion tour of the old place. Back then the grass was high and the brush all a tangle. Cousin Gene Bell had come to the reunion from Ohio, and luckily his growing-up years had been spent there in tiny Wybark, just up the road from Muskogee, which made Gene the ideal person to guide the tour of the Marshall Cemetery.

Once we were out of the cars and walking toward an apparent entrance, Gene grabbed a broken branch with which he began tapping the ground as we walked forward. His action seemed curious, so we inquired as to the why. He casually said, "Snakes don't have ears but they are sensitive to vibrations." He wanted to alert them to our presence. Overgrown and unkempt would best describe the cemetery, but this excursion was dedicated to finding and honoring our long-dead relatives, so snakes or no snakes, we were not to be deterred, whatever the difficulty in finding our people.

The memories of 1991 had imprinted the improbability that someone would choose such unfit ground for burial anytime in the future. But here we stood, gathered as family to bury another cousin, William Allen Glover. Thankfully, attention had been given those receiving grounds, now allowing a degree of honor for those buried therein.

As we waited for the graveside services to begin, a cousin approached me and asked, "Now, you're from Utah, is that right?" With those few words I knew what was coming next, and in all honesty, my back did straighten as I confirmed

FOREWORD

that I lived in Utah. I love being a Utahn, but experience had taught me to prepare for certain questions. "Isn't that where all those Mormons are?" Again I answered yes, which led to the expected, "Well, you're not one of them, are you?" Answering proudly that indeed I was, we had finally arrived at the trophy question: "I thought they didn't allow Blacks to be members?"

In that brief pause before William's graveside service began, I did my best to disabuse my cousin's thinking. Yes, I'm Black and a Latter-day Saint, or what he might call a "Mormon."

His questions, innocent as they were, weren't a surprise. As a Black member of The Church of Jesus Christ of Latter-day Saints, I had received and answered those same questions many times before. But somehow, standing solemnly among my kindred dead, it resonated with me how universal such experiences had been. If people knew next to nothing about Latter-day Saints, they knew we gathered in Utah—somewhere we had engaged in polygamy in past days—and that tenets of that faith were hostile to Blacks.

The experiences in Wybark occurred in the early 1990s. Later, in 1999, one of Salt Lake City's daily newspapers, the *Deseret News*, conducted a survey of its readership as the world prepared to enter a new century. The major question posed was, "What have been the greatest stories of the past 100 years?" The hands-down winner was the official revelation received by the Church leadership in 1978 allowing those of Black African ancestry to again become ordained in the Church's lay priesthood and again engage in temple attendance. Two world wars, the Spanish flu, the Great Depression, government challenges to monopolies, the Holocaust, atomic bombs, polio, Korea, the civil rights movement, Vietnam . . . the list extends endlessly, yet, for the readers of the Church News section of the *Deseret News*, all else was eclipsed by that one bit of news—steeped in race. I hasten to add that the significance was not limited to Latter-day Saints. The news of June 8, 1978, was so compelling that at least two commercial flights announced the event mid-flight. Such was the worldwide connection between race and The Church of Jesus Christ of Latter-day Saints.

No longer considered a regional faith, what has historically been known as "Mormonism" is now a dynamic, proselytizing religion with millions of members worldwide. It saddens me that we have yet to rid ourselves of views that have never been of God.

A recent anniversary marked my fifty-seventh year as a member of the faith.

I was converted to the Church of Jesus Christ in 1964. The location was Colorado Springs, Colorado, the city and state of my birth. In the summer of that year, I returned to live at my mother's home after briefly residing in Portland, Oregon.

The early sixties were a time of growing racial unrest in much of America, as Blacks, frustrated with the slow progress of civil rights, began voicing their concerns more openly and stridently. Race had always been an issue in America, but now in the sixties, the heat of the debate was rising.

My parents, Darius M. Gray (born late 1800s) and Elsie M. Johnson Gray (born early 1900s), came into this world and began their working years during a period of time when Negroes were allowed only menial jobs. Typically, "Coloreds" had few opportunities for education in those days. In the case of my father and mother, Dad had the greater education, having made it to the fifth grade, whereas Mom had only four years of schooling. But compared to many of their generation, they were fortunate.

Like most parents, Darius and Elsie yearned for better days and better opportunities for their children, if not to be experienced themselves. Somehow they held to a vision of what could be rather than what hadn't been. As their children, we were taught lessons centered on the value of education and how knowledge could open the door to possibilities, even for Coloreds. While Mom and Dad held to a positive vision of life, it was one of limited reach. College was seldom mentioned, but a high school education for their children was a must. My parents also placed great worth on moral truths and values. Through their examples, we were shown the benefits of respecting others as well as respecting ourselves.

They also had a strong sense of racial identity. They were proud of their ethnicity, its accomplishments, and their endurance in the face of so much adversity. This, too, they undertook to teach their children.

It was with this family background, and in the days enveloping the explosion of this country's inner cities centered on inequality, that I became a member of The Church of Jesus Christ of Latter-day Saints. The focus here is not my conversion to the faith, but the "how" and "when" of my becoming aware of the restriction on priesthood for Blacks. For an event that would figure so prominently in my life, it happened almost as an afterthought.

It was the night before my scheduled baptism. I was at the apartment of the two missionaries who were conducting my pre-baptismal interview when the issue was raised. The subject of race, which is evident throughout the Book of Mormon, had come up once before. That first inquiry resulted in my being told that we would get to the matter later. Now, the night before I was to be baptized, "later" arrived.

I asked, "As I read about the Lamanites in the Book of Mormon, I see that they had dark skin and were often out of favor with God. How, if in any way, does this relate to me?"

Both missionaries were seated on the couch. One stood and walked over to the corner, leaving his companion to respond. There was a pause. "Well, Brother Gray," said the missionary, "the primary implication is that you won't be able to hold the priesthood." Then he went about explaining that this restriction was because of my race.

Having two young men, supposedly representatives of God, tell me that my race would disqualify me from holding the priesthood was more than I was willing to accept. By then I knew the worth and power of that priesthood, and all of my prior training had declared my right as an equal to any other man—including those Latter-day Saint men and boys who held that priesthood. That night as I left the missionaries' apartment, I knew there would be one less baptism taking place the coming day.

Back at home, the newly disclosed restriction continued to torment me. Earlier in the discussions I had received a testimony of the restored gospel, but self-respect—or loyalty to my upbringing—now challenged that testimony. Finally, in desperation, I sought God's guidance on a dilemma that I could not resolve alone. In His infinite wisdom, a generous Father explicitly confirmed that this was the restored gospel and that I was to join. No mention was given whether the restriction was of God or of man, whether it was right or wrong. The following day, knowing full well that I would be restricted in my membership, I was baptized into The Church of Jesus Christ of Latter-day Saints.

This foreword is being written in support of the book *Let's Talk about Race and Priesthood*, authored by W. Paul Reeve, a dear friend who just happens to be the preeminent scholar and historian most steeped in the details of our shared faith's history in matters of race. I can think of no one better equipped to guide your unfolding journey.

I've had the honor of knowing and interacting with many marvelous scholars of the topic, but none does it better than Paul Reeve. About the only thing to impress me more than his scholarship is his heart, which is guided by the restored gospel of Christ and the truths it offers. The journey you undertake when reading this book will be fraught with eye-opening a-ha moments, often followed by feelings of disbelief and maybe a few tears. Trust me—it will all be for your good, and therefore worth the resulting road rash.

In Closing

Today I found myself reflecting back to a particular sacrament meeting that took place in the late 1960s. It was at a University of Utah married students' ward, and on that Sunday we were seated in the chapel's center section, about midway back from the front, with me on the aisle. When the sacrament tray was presented, I partook of the bread and then reached for the handle to pass the tray to those seated at my right, including my wife. I was stunned as the tray was quickly pulled away, only to have the elder reach around me and offer the sacrament to my melanin-deprived wife, who then passed it onward. Eye contact was made with this brother in the gospel, and his expression left no doubt about his motive. My cursed hand would not be allowed to handle the Lord's Supper.

An area not often considered is the sense of isolation that can accompany Black membership. I felt it that Sunday even though no words were exchanged; a look and brief action bore witness to my aloneness. That same reality can afflict members of color even today. Though minority membership blossomed following the revelation of 1978, for some there remain old judgments steeped in curses, worthiness, and lack of valiance.

Senior leaders of The Church of Jesus Christ of Latter-day Saints have often affirmed the belief that the hand of God was instrumental in bringing forth this great nation along with a constitution that focused on the individual. They have held that America was intended by God to be a beacon of freedom and truth. How odd then that racism and the embrace of slavery have corrupted every portion of these hallowed lands. Throughout history both the nation and its people have been at cross purposes. Would concepts of inclusion and dedication to Deity hold sway, or would hatred and greed seize the day?

Our focus must not be on history alone or the shortcomings of humankind, as there is good news, even great news, if we will but embrace it. God is alive in His heaven, and continuing revelations guide our paths.

The Church Today

In theology and practice, The Church of Jesus Christ of Latter-day Saints embraces the universal human family.

FOREWORD

> Latter-day Saint scripture and teachings affirm that God loves all of His children and makes salvation available to all. God created the many diverse races and ethnicities and esteems them all equally. As the Book of Mormon puts it, "all are alike unto God." [2 Nephi 26:33] . . .
>
> Today, the Church disavows the theories advanced in the past that black skin is a sign of divine disfavor or curse, or that it reflects unrighteous actions in a premortal life; that mixed-race marriages are a sin; or that blacks or people of any other race or ethnicity are inferior in any way to anyone else. Church leaders today unequivocally condemn all racism, past and present, in any form.[1]

The above comments are but a small portion of the Church's essay "Race and the Priesthood," the official statement that strives to lift the institution and its members from a troubling racial history. Reflecting nearly thirty years to that day at the Wybark cemetery with my cousin who had thought the Church racist, we have come a long way. Major events in the nation, and within the Church, have necessitated honest examinations of our past, and of our hearts. Becoming disciples of Christ holds within it the expectation of changed attitudes and behaviors. As my dear friend Catherine Stokes, herself a pioneer, has said, "This is the United States of America, where you are free to hate anyone you choose. That is until you take upon yourself the name of Christ. At which point the right to hate is no longer available to you."

DARIUS A. GRAY
January 2022

INTRODUCTION

In 1909, Nelson Holder Ritchie and his wife Annie Cowan Russell approached their bishop, John M. Whitaker, in the hope of obtaining temple recommends. Annie, 52, had converted to The Church of Jesus Christ of Latter-day Saints in Great Bend, Kansas, in 1890, while Nelson, 69, joined after the family moved to Utah, where he was baptized in 1892. The couple's two oldest daughters had each been sealed in the Salt Lake Temple, and now Annie and Nelson wanted the same blessing for themselves.[1]

Nelson was a Civil War veteran who had opened a hotel and livery stable in Great Bend following the war. William C. Mann and Willard Richard Johnson, two missionaries from the Church, took room and board at the Ritchie hotel and soon became friends with the couple and their young children. The Ritchie family's conversion and subsequent move to Utah followed. It was a typical conversion experience, except for what happened when Nelson and Annie applied for temple admission. They were denied—not because Bishop Whitaker decided that they lacked devotion, but because he deemed Nelson racially ineligible.[2]

Nelson had in fact formerly been enslaved. He was the child of a relationship that was most likely not consensual, with a white father and Black enslaved mother. Nelson escaped from slavery, and by 1891, when Latter-day Saint missionaries began staying at the Ritchie hotel, he was a prominent businessman in the city. The first time that Elder Mann met Nelson, Mann described him as "a dark man" who "dont belong to the church but he treats us veary kind." In contrast, Mann described Annie as white.[3]

In 1909, when Nelson sought a temple recommend, his

race dominated the discussion—not his devotion to God. As Bishop Whitaker later recalled, Nelson had been a "faithful and a good provider" and he "saw no reason why he could not" go to the temple, except for one problem: "As soon as [Nelson] crossed the thresh hold of the front door, I felt that he had negro blood in him." Whitaker "asked many questions concerning [Nelson's] birth" and subsequently interviewed Annie in order to learn "all the facts she knew," yet he still "felt the same."[4]

Nelson and Annie "were really disturbed over the matter" and noted that two of their daughters had already been sealed in the temple. Whitaker, nonetheless, refused to budge. He told them that he "appreciated they were good saints" but "feeling as I did, I dare not issue a recommend to the temple unless my feeling changed." According to his "understanding of the gospel anyone with Negro Blood was not entitled to the temple rights." Whitaker called the case "a source of considerable sorrow" to him because, he said, "I believe they were good saints." Nonetheless, he "never gave the recommend."[5]

In the October 2020 general conference, President Russell M. Nelson taught eternal truths that do not match the treatment given to Nelson and Annie Ritchie in 1909. President Nelson said that "each of us has a divine potential because each is a child of God. Each is equal in His eyes." He then explained that "the implications of this truth are profound." He asked us to "listen carefully" to what he was about to say: "God does not love one race more than another. His doctrine on this matter is clear. He invites all to come unto Him, 'black and white, bond and free, male and female'" (2 Nephi 26:33). "I assure you," President Nelson continued, "that your standing before God is not determined by the color of your skin. Favor or disfavor with God is dependent upon your devotion to God and His commandments and not the color of your skin."[6]

Nelson Holder Ritchie's bishop, in contrast, refused Nelson a temple recommend because of the color of his skin. Despite

INTRODUCTION

Annie Cowan Russell and Nelson Holder Ritchie

such a difficult rejection, Nelson remained committed to his faith. He died in 1913, in Sugar House, Salt Lake City, when he was seventy-two years old.[7]

Following Nelson's death, recollections of his racial identity faded. Church policy did not allow people of African descent to receive priesthood ordinations and temple rituals, even by proxy after death.[8] Yet the Ritchie family proved how impossible it was to enforce such a policy among the living, let alone among the dead. Annie waited ten years and then went to the Salt Lake Temple, where Nelson was given the priesthood by proxy in 1923 and the endowment ritual on the same day. Annie then had Nelson sealed to her by proxy in 1924, also in the Salt Lake Temple.[9]

The family's children followed a similar path. They married white spouses and passed as white. In fact, all nine of the couple's children that survived into adulthood received temple rituals and priesthood ordination, either in life or by proxy after death, before June 1978 when revelation reversed the nearly 130-year-old ban.[10]

Nelson and Annie's youngest son, Russell Dewey Ritchie, offers an intriguing example. He was eleven years old when his parents were prevented from entering the temple. There is no indication as to what he understood about the situation or how Bishop Whitaker approached Russell the following year when he turned twelve and was eligible to be ordained a deacon. Records indicate that Russell participated in Sunday School and the Young Men's Mutual Improvement Association but that he was not ordained to the priesthood. It is possible that Bishop Whitaker used the same reasoning to prevent Russell's ordination that he had used to bar his parents from the temple.[11]

Russell eventually moved to California, where he became a pharmacist and married Lois Meyer in 1931 at the Methodist Episcopal Church in Orange County. The couple had one child, a son, Donald, who married his wife at the Knox Presbyterian Church in Inglewood, California, in 1962. By 1970, however, Russell had returned to the faith of his youth.[12]

Surviving sources do not indicate what prompted the return, but Russell began attending the Holly Park Ward in Inglewood. There is no indication of what explanation Russell offered for his lack of ordination or what questions his bishop, Donald Richard Kemp, asked. Sources do indicate that on March 29, 1970, Bishop Kemp ordained Russell a deacon. He was seventy-one years old when he finally received the priesthood more typically given at age twelve. Every two to three months thereafter, Kemp ordained Russell to succeeding priesthood offices: teacher, then priest, and finally, on November 15, 1970, just shy of his seventy-second birthday, Russell received the Melchizedek Priesthood and became an elder.[13]

In 1972, Russell attended the Los Angles temple, where he was sealed by proxy to his mother and father, an ordinance denied his parents sixty-three years earlier. His sister Grace traveled to Los Angeles to be with him and served as proxy for their mother when Russell was sealed to their parents.[14]

Descendants of Nelson Holder Ritchie and his wife Annie Cowan Russell continue to exhibit African ancestry in their DNA even though they look white. According to Church policies in place before 1978, their ancestry should have prevented their priesthood ordination and temple admission. Because they passed as white, however, they were admitted into priesthood and temples based on their "devotion to God and His commandments" while their father and mother had been barred because of the color of their father's skin.[15]

The Ritchie family story illustrates the challenges of defining race. Is it skin color? Physical characteristics? Something biological in a person's blood? Or is race simply something human beings have invented in their minds to distinguish between people who look like them and people who look different? Is race an invention of the human mind, used across the long course of history to justify discrimination, violence, enslavement, extermination, genocide, and other such atrocities, when in reality we are biologically brothers and sisters, children of heavenly parents who honor the diversity of their human family?[16]

God gave each of us agency, including His prophets, and allows us to exercise it in ways that produce divisions among us. He has commanded us to exercise our agency to increase feelings of love, especially across cultural, religious, racial, and ethnic divides. He weeps when we use our agency to discriminate.

The history that follows is a burden on the body of Christ, but one that can become light if we join together to lift it, to carry its weight, to sit with the heaviness of it all, and to ponder on its implications and its messiness. This history is heavy, but when we take upon ourselves the yoke of Christ, in His meek and humble heart we can "find rest" for our souls (Matthew 11:29).

If we can pull a handcart to connect with the sacrifices of our white pioneer ancestors, then we can load that same handcart with the heaviness of racism and feel its weight as we struggle up the hills of prejudice, past and present, that President Russell M. Nelson has invited us to climb.[17] We can cross the Sweetwater River time and time again to carry the racism that Black Latter-day Saint pioneers endured in the nineteenth and twentieth centuries and continue to endure in the twenty-first. In Christ the yoke of racism and burden of hate can become light, especially as we seek solace in Him, the one who is the God of "all flesh" and declares Himself "mighty to save" (D&C 133:25, 47).

Every shade of flesh belongs to the Lord, and collectively those shades are strong enough to carry the burden of this history. My experience as a Latter-day Saint is that when we lift together we become "true and living"; we bear one another's burdens that they might become light (D&C 1:30; see also Mosiah 18:8). We mourn with Annie Cowan Russell and Nelson Holder Ritchie through the injustice of being barred from the temple in 1909 and rejoice with Russell Dewey Ritchie at the joy of being sealed to his parents in 1972. This book is an invitation to share in the lifting, that collectively the burden of racism might become light.

Our heavenly parents weep when we as their children fail to get along. Joseph Smith describes this very thing in the book of Moses: The prophet Enoch questions God about what makes Him weep, especially because God is "holy, and from all eternity to all eternity." What could possibly make an eternal God cry, Enoch wonders? "How is it thou canst weep?" (Moses 7:29, 31).

In reply, "the Lord said unto Enoch: Behold these thy brethren; they are the workmanship of mine own hands, and I gave unto them their knowledge, in the day I created them; and in the Garden of Eden, gave I unto man his agency." Along with agency, the Lord gave His children commandments "that they should love one another, and that they should choose me, their Father" (Moses 7:32–33). Rather than exercising their agency to love one another, however, God explains that His children are sometimes "without affection, and they hate their own blood" (Moses 7:33). That is what makes God weep.

This book is mostly about what makes God weep.

INTRODUCTION

• • •

As I have come to understand it, the history of the racial priesthood and temple restrictions in The Church of Jesus Christ of Latter-day Saints is best understood in three phases. During the first phase there were no barriers. Church leaders ordained Black men to the priesthood, and temple admission policies included people "of every color."[18] Over the course of the nineteenth century, however, the open racial vision of the founding decades gave way, in fits and starts, to a second phase, which barred priesthood ordination and temple admission from people of Black African descent. In the work that follows, I will show how these policies, which lasted for roughly 130 years, were sometimes referred to as doctrines, were inconsistently applied, and were not in harmony with the scriptural mandates of the founding years.

In June 1978, President Spencer W. Kimball received a revelation that returned the Church to its universal roots and restored what was lost—priesthood and temple admission to people of African descent. This third phase did not mark something new as much as it reestablished a commitment to the founding principles of the Restoration. Phase three reconfirmed the Church's original universalism, that the human family in all of its diversity is equal in God's sight, that Jesus Christ claims "all flesh" as His own, that He is "no respecter of persons" (D&C 1:34–35; 38:16), and that "all men are privileged the one like unto the other, and none are forbidden" (2 Nephi 26:28).

PHASE ONE

UNIVERSAL PRIESTHOOD AND TEMPLES

CHAPTER 1

BLACK CONVERTS IN THE U.S. NORTH

"Unto every creature"

The first person of Black African ancestry to join the Church of Christ (renamed the Church of the Latter-day Saints in 1834 and The Church of Jesus Christ of Latter-day Saints in 1838) was a formerly enslaved man named Peter who began worshipping with the Saints at Kirtland, Ohio, after missionaries passed through the region in November 1830. It was just seven months after the founding of the Church, and there have been Black Latter-day Saints ever since.[1]

The scriptures of the Restoration are filled with examples of the universal nature of the restored gospel and the divine mandate early Saints received to share it widely. Nephi promised that "all the earth" would "see the salvation of the Lord" and that "every nation, kindred, tongue and people shall be blessed" (1 Nephi 19:17). It was a common refrain throughout Latter-day Saint scripture. In case there was any room for doubt, Joseph Smith received five revelations that were even more specific. The Lord instructed him in August 1831 that "the gospel must be preached unto every creature, with signs following them that believe" (D&C 58:64). It was a message that the Lord repeated in November of the same year, twice more in 1832, and again in 1837 (see D&C 68:8; 80:1; 84:62; 112:28).

"Every creature" left no one out. Any notion that the gospel and its priesthood and temple privileges were to be shared in stages—white people first and then Black people—ignores these revelations and represents an after-the-fact justification for the racial restrictions. It erases from Latter-day Saint history the lives and contributions of Black pioneers. Historians have found no racial barriers against baptism, priesthood ordination, or temple admission in the first two decades of the Restoration.[2] In fact, the opposite is true. There is abundant evidence that Joseph Smith taught a sweeping vision of inclusion.

In 1832, missionary Ezekiel Roberts preached in Cincinnati, Ohio, to a man named Elijah Able. In September of that year, Able accepted baptism from Roberts, a decision that would transform Able's life and thereafter move it in unexpected directions. He and his wife Mary Ann Adams would go on to preside over a multigenerational family of Latter-day Saints and directly influence the Church's racial trajectory, especially because he is the most well-documented Black priesthood holder in the early Church. Even more remarkable, his son and grandson would also be ordained to the priesthood, one in 1871 and the other in 1935 (the latter after passing as white).[3]

Able is consistently listed in U.S. Census records as either "quadroon" or "mulatto," indicating that he likely had a lighter complexion than some African Americans.[4] Nonetheless, he was legally Black according to prevailing racial standards in the United States, and unlike some people of mixed racial ancestry, he did not pass as white. He was understood to be "colored" throughout his life, including in Latter-day Saint records. At the end of his life, a Salt Lake County death record included the word "colored" in the column where health officials typically entered the name of a close relative.[5] Able thus represents the possibilities and the promises of universal male priesthood ordination and the dignifying doctrine that the entire human family is "alike unto God" (2 Nephi 26:33).

Within four years of his baptism, Able would receive priesthood ordination as well as access to all of the temple rituals then available. Ambrose Palmer, the presiding elder at New Portage, Ohio, ordained Able an elder on January 25, 1836.[6] Joseph Smith signed Able's ministerial certificate two months later substantiating that fact.[7] Joseph Smith Sr. gave Able his patriarchal blessing, noting that Able was "ordained an Elder" and that he was "anointed" to be secured "against the power of the destroyer."[8] Alvah Beman and Ruben Hedlock administered Able's washing and anointing ceremonies in Kirtland in 1836.[9]

By the end of 1836, Zebedee Coltrin, a president of the Seventy, ordained Able a member of the Third Quorum of Seventy.[10] Able remained a committed member of that missionary quorum for the rest of his life. He served three missions, the last one in 1883 when he was seventy-five years old. One of his proselytes from an earlier mission, a woman named Eunice Kinney, recalled the power of his preaching: "The Spirit rested upon him and he preached a most powerful sermon. It was such a Gospel sermon as I had never heard before, and I felt in my heart that he was one of God's chosen ministers."[11] Able's own life thus demonstrates that there were no racial barriers to priesthood ordination or temple rituals as the Restoration began.

In 1843, after Able had moved back to Cincinnati, Ohio, Church leaders advised him to limit his preaching to the "coloured population." At a Cincinnati branch conference that year, Apostle John E. Page commented that "he respects a coloured Bro, as such, but wisdom forbids that we should introduce [him] before the public." Able responded that "he had no disposition to force himself upon an equality with white people," and the conference advised him to limit his preaching to Black people.[12] Church leaders thus understood Able to be "coloured" and a priesthood holder. Their concerns were over who he preached to, not over the fact that a Black man held the priesthood.

Q. Walker Lewis, an abolitionist and leader in the Black community in Boston and Lowell, Massachusetts, also received the priesthood. William Smith, Joseph Smith's younger brother and an Apostle at the time, ordained him an elder in 1843 or 1844. Several Church leaders, including Ezra T. Benson, Wilford Woodruff, William Smith, and Brigham Young, visited Lowell over the next few years and saw nothing out of the ordinary in Lewis's ordination.[13] In November 1844, for example, Wilford Woodruff described Lewis as a "coloured Brother who was an Elder."[14] Woodruff maintained correspondence with Lewis with no hint of concern over his status as a Black priesthood holder.[15] Lewis in turn was a committed Latter-day Saint who paid a generous tithe and hosted missionaries who preached in his home.[16]

Other Black men converted in the early decades of the Restoration, but not all of them were ordained to the priesthood. That, however, was nothing out of the ordinary. Not all white men were ordained, either, and no enslaved men were ordained in the South.[17] In the nineteenth century, the purpose of ordination was to provide each congregation with leadership, not to ensure that all men held priesthood office. In 1842, the branch in Brandywine, Pennsylvania, for example, reported 124 total members, which included seven elders, two priests, three teachers, and two deacons, while the branch in Salem, Massachusetts, counted 66 members, with one elder and one priest.[18] Not until the early decades of the twentieth century did the Church systematically ordain young men to priesthood offices.[19] The fact that a few Black men were ordained to the priesthood when white men were not universally ordained makes it that much more remarkable.

Elsewhere in the North, missionaries cast a wide net. In October 1842, missionary Charles Wesley Wandell preached at New Canaan, Connecticut, and found a receptive audience. Jane Elizabeth Manning, a religious seeker who had joined the New Canaan Congregational Church just the year before, was still looking for "something more." When Wandell delivered his message, Manning became "fully convinced that it was the true Gospel he presented and [she] must embrace it." She was baptized on October 14, 1842, and her life was thereafter shaped by the Latter-day Saint movement. She in turn shaped the Church that she embraced in ways atypical for the average convert.[20]

Manning's enthusiasm for the Latter-day Saint gospel

quickly spread among other family members. As her brother Isaac later recalled, Jane "heard the Gospel and was baptized and soon after she got . . . the whole family to be baptized."[21] Isaac and his wife Lucinda, his sister Sarah and her husband Anthony Stebbins, his sister Angeline, and the matriarch of the group, Philles Eliza Manning Treadwell, all converted, likely by December 1842.[22] In May 1843, six of the seven new converts donated a combined $1.12½ as a tithe offering to their Norwalk Connecticut branch.[23] By the end of 1843, the family had migrated to Nauvoo to join the main body of Saints.[24]

Because they were Black, the family was denied passage at Buffalo, New York, on the same ship that carried white Latter-day Saints. As a result, they were forced to walk the rest of the way, a nearly thousand-mile journey on foot. As Jane later recalled, "our feet became sore and cracked open and bled until you could see the whole print of our feet with blood on the ground." Yet, she relied on the collective faith of her family to sustain her. "We stopped and united in prayer to the Lord," she explained. "We asked God the Eternal Father to heal our feet and our prayers were answered and our feet were healed forthwith."[25] At Nauvoo, Joseph and Emma Smith welcomed the family into the Nauvoo Mansion House, where they recovered from their arduous journey.

"Come in all of you," Jane remembered Emma saying. She called for Joseph Smith, who also greeted the family and reassured them. "God bless you, you are among friends now and you will be protected."[26] Emma and Joseph Smith invited the Manning and Stebbins families to stay at the Mansion House for a week while they sought permanent accommodations. The Smiths employed Jane as servant and laundress and hired her brother Isaac as chef. Later in life Isaac recalled, "I was a cook in the prophet's kitchen at Nauvoo, and he used to say I was a mighty good cook too. I cooked the prophet's meals . . . when I was servant in the family."[27]

The warm welcome the Manning and Stebbins families

received and the generosity the Smiths extended to them remained with some of the family for the rest of their lives. In 1899, in fact, when the *Salt Lake Herald* interviewed Isaac Manning, he remembered the way Joseph Smith had treated them over fifty years earlier. He recounted the "prophet's goodness to them when they arrived in Nauvoo, almost perfect strangers" and noted that Joseph Smith "treated them to the best his house afforded."[28]

More than the generosity they received, it was a sense of Smith's prophetic mantle that won their devotion. Jane claimed to have seen Smith in vision back in Connecticut so that when she first met him in Nauvoo she said, "I was certain he was a prophet because I knew it."[29] Her sister Sarah expressed a similar sentiment throughout her life. She was fond of saying, "You can just as easily make me believe that the sun never shone as that Joseph was not a prophet of God."[30] Isaac likewise told a fellow Latter-day Saint that "he knew Brother Joseph was a man of God, and he would have laid down his life for the prophet if he could have done so."[31]

When Joseph and Hyrum Smith were murdered in June 1844, the Mannings were devastated. "I shall never forget that time of agony and sorrow," Jane wrote.[32] In the wake of the tragedy, the sexton at Nauvoo turned to Isaac for help. Isaac dug two graves in the Nauvoo cemetery as decoys to protect the bodies from desecration, and caskets loaded with sand were buried following a public ceremony. Manning then dug two additional graves in the southwest corner of Joseph and Emma's homestead, where the bodies were actually buried.[33]

Isaac's service in behalf of the two men whom he revered remained a source of satisfaction to him for the rest of his life. This important memory was such an intimate connection to Joseph and Hyrum Smith that in 1903 he signed a statement declaring with honor, "I dug the graves."[34]

The Prophet Joseph Smith thus personally modeled an inclusive vision for the Zion society that his revelations articulated. He recorded five revelations between 1831 and 1837 instructing him that the gospel was to be preached "unto every creature." The Book of Mormon likewise declared that Jesus Christ did not do anything except it was "for the benefit of the world," no exclusions: "For he loveth the world, even that he layeth down his own life that he may draw *all men* unto him. Wherefore, he commandeth *none* that they shall not partake of his salvation" (2 Nephi 26:24; emphasis added). These were messages early Saints took seriously as they shared the good news of the Restoration. The Zion society they hoped to build was presided over by a Savior who declared "all flesh is mine, and I am no respecter of persons" (D&C 38:16), an ideal that at least some of His followers sought to emulate.

CHAPTER 2

BLACK CONVERTS IN THE U.S. SOUTH

"Altho in bondage . . . yet I kept the faith"

In the South, Latter-day Saint missionaries also spread their message without regard to race. They baptized white enslavers as well as their Black enslaved. At least twenty-six enslaved people (likely more but record keeping was spotty) converted to the Church before the Thirteenth Amendment to the Constitution outlawed slavery in 1865.

Despite burdens not of their own making, some enslaved converts followed the westward trajectory of their new faith alongside their enslavers. John Burton, baptized in the 1830s in Missouri along with his enslavers John and Susan McCord Burton, is one example. Susan was left a widow in 1838 with two young children. John Burton, her enslaved man who was about forty-one years old, helped Susan and her young family move to Illinois, where he joined with fellow Saints in building Nauvoo.[1] In April 1845, he paid $1.00 cash tithing, a contribution that was entered into a ledger book as a donation from "Widow Susan Burton's (Negro John)."[2]

Susan Burton married Joseph Lee Robinson as a plural wife in Nauvoo, and John Burton migrated to Winter Quarters with the family and drove one of Robinson's wagons on the overland trail from Illinois. Robinson described Burton as "a colored man, a member of the Church which was the property of my second wife—a good and faithful servant."[3] Robinson also called Burton "a good Saint," a description that other sources substantiate.[4] At Winter Quarters, Burton lived next to Green Flake, a fellow enslaved Latter-day Saint. Burton survived the difficult winter of 1846 and 1847 wherein over 700 Saints died from privation and harsh conditions.[5] He received tithing credit that winter for digging the grave of one of those who had died.⁶

From Winter Quarters Burton made the overland trek to Utah in 1847. His enslavers sent him ahead to plant crops and prepare a shelter for them to live in when they arrived the following year. Robinson was subsequently called to settle southern Utah and took Burton with him. Burton thus helped build the new town of Parowan. In 1861, when leaders there decided to erect a proper meetinghouse for worship, Burton donated $15.00.⁷ It was the smallest monetary contribution recorded in the clerk's ledger but, like the widow's mite, it represented a sacrifice greater than those who donated out of their abundance (see Mark 12:41–44).

Burton received two patriarchal blessings, one in 1850 and another in 1854. He told both patriarchs that he believed he was born in 1797 in Campbell County, Virginia, to a father named Zacharia and a mother named Jenny, but that is all he knew about his parents.⁸ If he had siblings, there is no indication that he was aware of them. Slavery robbed him of his birth family and also deprived him of the chance to marry and create a family of his own. As Frederick Douglass, the renowned abolitionist who was himself formerly enslaved, put it, "Slavery does away with fathers as it does away with families."⁹

Burton died in Utah within a decade of Congress freeing enslaved people in all U.S. territories. He had been a Latter-day Saint for over thirty years by that time, and he had shared in the difficult labor of building four frontier communities: Nauvoo, Winter Quarters, Salt Lake City, and Parowan. He gave his labor and his cash to create an inclusive vision of Zion, one without racial barriers, and he did so while being enslaved.¹⁰

Evidence suggests that enslaved people like John Burton were baptized of their own accord. In fact, in cases where white Latter-day Saints enslaved more than one person, there is no situation where all enslaved people were baptized, an indication that the enslaved were not forced to follow their enslavers into the faith. There are also examples of enslaved people who were baptized before their enslavers or independently of them, further evidence that enslavers did not require baptism of their enslaved.[11]

While baptism may have been a choice, the ability to decide how to practice their faith after baptism was limited among the enslaved. In most cases, enslaved Latter-day Saints were enslaved to fellow members of their faith who were at liberty to sell them and even separate them from their families if financial or other circumstances changed.[12] The choice to move west with the Latter-day Saint migration to the Great Basin was also out of an enslaved person's control. If white enslavers migrated west, their enslaved people had no choice to stay behind with family and friends even if they wanted. In 1847 or 1848, for example, John Brown or his wife Elizabeth Crosby Brown purchased an enslaved girl named Betsy in either Missouri or Mississippi. They did so because Elizabeth Crosby Brown had grown up with enslaved people caring for her and thus "did not know how to work." Betsy would do the work for her.[13]

Betsy was eleven years old when the Browns took her from whatever family she may have known. She became a part of the 1848 Latter-day Saint overland trek to what would become Utah Territory. In 1855, at age eighteen, she accepted baptism into the faith, in Lehi, Utah, where her enslavers had settled. Two years later John Brown listed Betsy as an "African Servant Girl" on a consecration deed he prepared and valued her at $1,000. Such 1850s deeds were symbolic. They were created as a way of demonstrating one's willingness to live the law of consecration without ever being required to give up one's possessions.[14] No property exchanged hands. Betsy, nonetheless, was listed among Brown's assets along with his oxen, cows, calves, potatoes, wheat, and corn and assigned a monetary value.[15] Two months later, Brown rebaptized Betsy with no apparent hint of irony at the juxtaposition of the consecration deed and the rebaptism.[16]

Betsy thus became a Utah pioneer but not by choice. Her

Amanda and Samuel Chambers

pioneer journey meant separation from her biological family, never to see her mother and father again. For a faith deeply centered on binding families together, some members of the faith became so enmeshed in enslavement that they failed to contemplate their own roles in pulling families apart.[17]

In contrast to Betsy's experience, if an enslaver did not migrate west, an enslaved person had no option to do so of their own volition. Samuel Chambers, for example, converted in 1844 in Mississippi at age thirteen. There were no organized branches in the area, and his enslaver did not convert. Chambers was thus alone in his religion, a one-man congregation who nourished a spark of faith in isolation for over twenty years. As he later recalled, "Altho in bondage for 20 years after receiving the gospel, yet I kept the faith."[18] On another occasion, he said, "I was baptized in the year 1844 and after that I was 21 years in bondage, during which time I never heard a word of the gospel." Even still, he explained, "The spirit of God remained within me. In 1865 I was liberated. I then commenced to save means to gather. This took me 4 years."[19]

By 1870, Chambers had saved enough money to migrate to Salt Lake City with his wife Amanda.[20] The Chamberses first lived in the Salt Lake Eighth Ward, where Samuel was appointed "assistant Deacon," although not ordained. Deacons in the nineteenth century primarily consisted of adults and were responsible for caring for meetinghouses. Chambers regularly attended deacons quorum meetings and there bore testimony.[21]

In August 1873, Chambers told his fellow deacons that he had "been 29 years in the church" and had "never been dissatisfied yet." On another occasion he announced, "I don't get tired of being with the Latter-day Saints, nor of being one of them. I'm glad that I ever took upon me the name of Christ."[22] A deep sense of humility permeates his testimonies. Chambers took his calling as a deacon seriously and relished the opportunity to contribute. On one occasion he explained, "Some think it is small to be a deacon," but then countered that "I think there is nothing small in the kingdom of God."[23]

In sum, the experiences of enslaved Latter-day Saints varied from person to person, and like every other aspect of their lives, their ability to respond to religious yearnings was not fully in their control. Slavery violated agency, a fundamental Latter-day Saint tenet, and it removed an enslaved person's choices. It crushed an enslaved person's economic, social, and political potential, and most significantly, it tore families apart. In fact, in 1833 the Lord declared to Joseph Smith that he granted "moral agency" unto His children so that "every man may be accountable for his own sins in the day of judgment. Therefore, it is not right that any man should be in bondage one to another" (D&C 101:78–79). The southern slave system, in contrast, was grounded in an evil ideology that asserted white superiority as its foundation and used violence, rape, and intimidation as its methods of control.

Latter-day Saint missionaries nonetheless cast a wide net as they preached "unto every creature." Enslaved people were invited into the fold alongside their enslavers. As the Book of Mormon declared, "bond and free" were ultimately "alike unto God" (2 Nephi 26:33). White enslavers, in other words, were no better in God's eyes than the Black people whom they enslaved.

In 1874, Samuel Chambers reminded the deacons in the Salt Lake Stake of that very idea: "I was born in a condition of slavery, and received the gospel in that condition," he told them. The gospel "is not only to the Gentiles but also to the African, for I am of that race. The knowledge I received is from God," he declared. "I have my weaknesses in connection with all men," he admitted on another occasion, but "I pray that we may be as one to build up the Kingdom of God."[24] Like the revelations Joseph Smith received, Chambers's vision of a Zion society was one of unity and inclusion.

CHAPTER 3

RACE RELATIONS IN JACKSON COUNTY, MISSOURI

"We have no special rule in the church, as to people of color"

Latter-day Saint newspaper editor William Wines Phelps touched off an unintended firestorm in Jackson County, Missouri, in July 1833 when he published a column simply titled "Free People of Color."[1] The leader of his faith, Joseph Smith, had recently defined Jackson County as a gathering place for his envisioned holy city, a Zion society where all would be welcome and there would be "no poor among them" (Moses 7:18). In addition to the conversion of Black people in the North and the South, both bond and free, Latter-day Saint leaders made it clear in their statements and in their actions that the message of the Restoration was inclusive. That inclusive vision, however, was not always welcome in a broader American society that was sorting out issues of race, slavery, and freedom all its own.

In this regard, it is important to remember that the Church of Jesus Christ was born into a fraught American racial context. The United States Constitution began with three important words, "We the people," but the nation was still grappling with questions about which people counted as "the people." United States President Andrew Jackson signed the Indian Removal Act into law less than two months following the founding of the Church. The new law called for the removal of eastern tribes from their traditional homelands followed by forced relocation to Indian Territory on the western edge of Missouri. It was designed to solve what was called "the Indian problem" in the nineteenth century.[2]

Slavery, too, forced the young nation to confront one of its central paradoxes: a country established on the foundational principles that "all men are created equal" and enjoy certain "inalienable" rights such as "life, liberty, and the pursuit of happiness" was also a country grounded in slavery.[3] Northern states responded to the ideals of the Revolution to eradicate slavery either outright or with some version of gradual emancipation. Those who advocated gradual emancipation believed that slavery was wrong but wanted to appease enslavers by honoring what they considered to be their right to their property. When the British empire outlawed slavery in 1833, for example, it compensated enslavers (not their former slaves) from government funds.[4]

Gradual emancipation laws were designed to provide an orderly and measured end to slavery. White people sometimes expressed fears that four million freed Black people emancipated at once would have no means of support and would become an unwelcome burden on public coffers. The American economy could not absorb that many freed people at once, the gradualists contended, so it was better to slowly emancipate them. More significantly, many white people who may have disliked slavery still feared race mixing and suggested that immediately freeing the enslaved would destroy the social order and threaten the white race. Black men would rape and attack white women, they predicted, or marry them. In either case, race mixing would darken the white race and make it unfit for democracy.[5]

In the minds of many people in the nineteenth century, the young nation's experiment in self-rule was really what was at stake. Race existed as a hierarchy in the nineteenth century, with a certain brand of white people, Anglo-Saxons, at the top. Racial definitions were fluid and illogical and functioned as a system designed to create order and superiority out of the perceived disorder of the confluence of people who had gathered to the United States.[6]

"Race" was a loosely used word that sometimes referred

to nationality as well as skin color or even religion. It was sometimes used to denigrate immigrants such as the Irish who might have looked white but who did not act white in the minds of political leaders or social thinkers. In contrast, Anglo-Saxons had marched across Europe to Britain and from Britain to America, where they founded a new government based in principles of liberty and equality. They represented the triumph of Western civilization and by their very success demonstrated that only true white people (Anglo-Saxons) were capable of self-rule—or so some leaders argued.[7]

U.S. laws and political attitudes in the nineteenth century flowed from this basic premise. In 1790, for example, the first Congress of the new nation stipulated that to become a naturalized citizen, a person had to be free and white.[8] In 1848, Senator John C. Calhoun argued on the floor of the United States Senate that "ours sir is the government of a white race."[9] And the U.S. Supreme Court in its 1857 Dredd Scott decision concluded that Black people possessed no rights "which the white man was bound to respect."[10] The American system was built for a certain "race" of white people, in other words. If you did not match existing ideals, you were deemed unfit to participate in American democracy, or worse still, as with Black people and Native Americans, you were considered a threat to it.

Thus, in the minds of many social thinkers in the nineteenth century, slavery was a twofold problem: First, it held an entire class of people in bondage, a violation of the nation's founding ideals. But second, it was also a racial problem—that is, what does the nation do with formerly enslaved people once they were free? Just because a person opposed slavery, in other words, it did not automatically mean that she believed in racial equality. Freed Black people represented a perceived threat to the racial order.

What this meant in practice was that northern white people might participate in antislavery societies but did not want free Black people moving north and intermarrying among them.

They did not believe Black people were equal to white people or that Black people were capable of self-rule. Their solution was to send free Black people to Africa. In 1816, people of this persuasion formed the American Colonization Society, which was designed to solve both of the nation's slavery problems. They would first free the slaves and then send them to Africa in order to "remove them beyond the reach of mixture," in Thomas Jefferson's words.[11] The society organized a colony for freed slaves in Liberia, on the western coast of Africa, and actively advocated it as a solution to the nation's racial problem.[12] Colonization remained the majority Northern position up through the Civil War, with Abraham Lincoln as one of its adherents even into the early years of his presidency.[13]

However, less than nine months after Joseph Smith established the Church of Christ, the antislavery movement in the United States changed dramatically. A minority group of what were deemed radical abolitionists advocated for immediate emancipation and full Black equality. William Lloyd Garrison, a prominent leader in this movement, founded a newspaper named *The Liberator* and issued its first edition on January 1, 1831. Garrison attacked the American Colonization Society as anti-Christian and pointed to Northern prejudice against Black people as a barrier to equality.[14]

The colonizationists initially absorbed such blows but eventually struck back. They argued, among other things, that those who favored immediate abolition were really "amalgamationists" in disguise. They suggested that if a person wanted to free the enslaved and live among them rather than send them to Africa, then such a person ultimately favored race mixing. "Amalgamation" was the pre–Civil War word borrowed from metallurgy (meaning the mixing of metals) used to mean the mixing of races. In the 1830s, the number of antislavery societies that advocated immediate emancipation grew to include forty-seven organizations in ten states. A corresponding anti-abolitionist backlash followed.[15]

It was within this charged national context that W. W. Phelps published his fateful column, "Free People of Color," in *The Evening and the Morning Star*, the newspaper he edited in Jackson County, Missouri. Phelps's column was aimed at Black Latter-day Saints and was designed to educate them on the laws of the state of Missouri should they choose to gather with the rest of the Saints to Zion.[16]

In his own words, Phelps wrote his July 1833 column "to prevent any misunderstanding among the churches abroad, respecting Free people of color, who may think of coming to the western boundaries of Missouri, as members of the church." Phelps indicated that Missouri was a slave state and as such had laws designed to limit the ability of even free Black people to move freely in the state. "Slaves are real estate in this and other states," he noted, "and wisdom would dictate great care among the branches of the church of Christ, on this subject." Phelps quoted two sections of the Missouri state code in his column which stipulated that a Black person migrating to the state had to have papers to substantiate his or her status as a free Black person, otherwise they would be subject to ten lashes on a bare back and expulsion from the state.[17]

Phelps made it clear that there were no racial barriers in the Church, but there were in the state of Missouri: "So long as we have no special rule in the church, as to people of color, let prudence guide," he counseled. Phelps urged "prudence" so that Black Latter-day Saints did not run afoul of Missouri law. At the same time, he indicated that the call to gather to Zion included everyone. It is additional evidence, three years after the Church's founding, that racial restrictions were not in place from the beginning.[18]

Residents of Jackson County reacted with fear to Phelps's article. They suggested that the Latter-day Saints had invited free Black people to the area in order to incite a slave rebellion. Phelps attempted to control the backlash and quickly issued an "extra" edition of the *Star* in a futile effort at damage control. "Having learned with regret, that an article entitled

FREE PEOPLE OF COLOR, in the last number of the Star, has been misunderstood, we feel it duty bound to state, in this Extra, that our intention was not only to stop free people of color from emigrating to this state, but to prevent them from being admitted as members of the church." It was a desperate attempt on Phelps's part to quiet fears and was simply not true.[19]

The extra edition of the *Star* signaled a willingness on Phelps's part to distance white Church members from their Black brothers and sisters when charges of racial inclusion threatened the Church's image. When push came to shove, Phelps resorted to protecting the Church over the gospel's universal ideals. It was a pattern that other Church leaders would follow in future circumstances across the course of the nineteenth century. In Missouri, Phelps's retraction did little good.[20]

Prominent citizens of Jackson County formed a vigilance committee in order to mobilize opposition to the Latter-day Saints. The leaders of the committee described Phelps's initial column as "an indirect invitation to the free brethren of colour in Illinois, to come like the rest to the land of Zion." They dismissed the "extra" as a "weak attempt to quiet our apprehension" and called it "a poor compliment to our understandings."[21] Missourians declared themselves flatly unwilling "to receive into the bosom of our families, as fit companions for our wives and daughters the degraded and corrupted free negroes and mulattoes, that are now invited to settle among us." Outsiders thus projected their fear of race mixing onto the Latter-day Saints almost from the beginning.[22]

Some Missouri residents further complained that the Saints had "opened an asylum for rogues and vagabonds and free blacks," while others were concerned that the Saints promoted black "ascendancy over the whites."[23] The accusations, in other words, suggested that Latter-day Saints did not understand prevailing racial hierarchies and accepted the very people into their religious society that the rest of white America knew should be segregated and even enslaved.

Four days after Phelps's "extra" appeared in print, a crowd of Jackson County residents stormed his printing office and destroyed all remaining copies of the extra as well as the original July issue of the *Star*. They scattered Phelps's type and the press itself and demolished his office and home. They seized Bishop Edward Partridge and Charles Allen and hauled them to the town square, where they tarred and feathered them, a nineteenth-century ritual of violence that was meant to serve as a warning to those so treated. It marked the beginning of the Latter-day Saint expulsion from Jackson County. Before the end of the year, some 1,200 Latter-day Saints would be driven from their homes, charged, at least in part, with being too inclusive.[24]

CHAPTER 4

OUTSIDERS VIEW THE LATTER-DAY SAINTS RACIALLY

"As if he had been of a different color"

The expulsion from Jackson County was only the beginning of the Saints' trouble in Missouri. They would be forced out of Clay County in 1836 and the state of Missouri altogether in 1838. To justify such discrimination, outsiders throughout the nineteenth century looked in on the Latter-day Saints and suggested that they were not merely religiously different but racially different as well. In doing so, outsiders fabricated a shared group identity for the Saints with an associated list of negative characteristics.[1] In Missouri, for example, outsiders referred to them as "the very dregs of that society from which they came, lazy, idle and vicious."[2]

One late-nineteenth-century memoir recounted the Latter-day Saints' troubled sojourn in Missouri and used racialized language to describe the experience. The author was a Missourian who had lived through the expulsion of the Saints from his state and remembered them unfavorably. He reported that they were "clannish, traded together, worked together, and carried with them a melancholy look." Their appearance was distinct enough "that one acquainted with them could tell a Mormon when he met him by the look upon his face almost as well as if he had been of a different color."[3]

Latter-day Saints recognized the way that they were racialized and spoke against it but to little avail. In Missouri, for example, apostle Parley P. Pratt complained that as the Saints were driven from their homes, most of the newspapers in the state described them as "Mormons, in contradistinction to the appellation of citizens, whites, &c., as if we had been some savage tribe, or some colored race of foreigners."[4] In Nauvoo, Elder Heber C. Kimball told an audience of Latter-day Saints, "We are not accounted as white people, and we don't want to live among them." He insisted, "I had rather live with the buffalo in the wilderness."[5]

In 1852, when Latter-day Saints openly announced that they practiced polygamy, it amplified public scorn.[6] The majority of Saints may have looked white and hailed from the United States and western Europe, but as outside observers claimed, they did not act white, and therefore they did not deserve to be treated like white people. They gave their free will over to the despots Joseph Smith and Brigham Young and they practiced polygamy, two things that marked them outside the bounds of whiteness and civilization. Rather than racial progress, they represented civilization's fearful decline, a plunge backward into barbarism and savagery.[7] Polygamy gave new life to the racially charged ways that outsiders imagined who Latter-day Saints were and sent them spiraling in new directions.[8]

By the 1860s, the medical community took note of the Latter-day Saints and argued that the practice of polygamy was giving rise to a degraded "new race" in the Great Basin. In 1860, Roberts Bartholow, a medical doctor, filed a report with the United States Senate in which he detailed his observations. According to Bartholow, children born to polygamous marriages were marked by a "striking uniformity in facial expression" which included "albuminous and gelatinous types of constitution" and "physical conformation" among "the young portion" of Latter-day Saints.[9]

Bartholow concluded that polygamy produced physical deformity in its offspring. It created "an expression of countenance and a style of feature, which may be styled the Mormon expression and style; an expression compounded of sensuality, cunning, suspicion, and smirking self-conceit. The yellow, sunken, cadaverous visage; the greenish-colored eyes; the thick, protuberant lips; the low forehead; the light, yellowish hair; and the lank, angular person, constitute an appearance so characteristic of the new race, the production of polygamy, as to distinguish them at a glance."[10] You could tell a Latter-day Saint when you saw one, Bartholow believed.

It was not only the medical community that imagined racial violations among the Latter-day Saints, but the Supreme Court of the United States did so as well. In 1879, in a unanimous decision, the Supreme Court rejected Latter-day Saint claims to polygamy as a religious principle protected by the First Amendment. The court ruled that the Constitution protected religious belief but not action. Latter-day Saints could believe in polygamy all they wanted, but they could not practice it.

Writing for the court, Chief Justice Morrison Waite justified his decision in part by using a racial argument. "Polygamy has always been odious among the northern and western nations of Europe," he argued, "and, until the establishment of the Mormon Church, was almost exclusively a feature of the life of Asiatic and of African people." In practicing polygamy, in other words, Latter-day Saints violated the standards of what it meant to be white and European.[11]

A fear of race mixing animated concern across the nation over polygamy, especially as outsiders imagined the consequences of a sexual merger between two of America's undesirable groups, Black people and Latter-day Saints. "The days of the white race are numbered in this country," the *St. Louis Globe Democrat* predicted in 1883. "North America will be another African continent inside of two centuries." At the crux of this fearful deterioration was the "American of the future"—"a black Mormon."[12]

As outsiders projected racial decline onto the Latter-day Saints, Latter-day Saint leaders in turn attempted to claim whiteness for themselves, a way to reassure a suspicious nation that they were white and acceptable just like the white Protestant majority. The most significant way to claim acceptance in the nineteenth century was in distance from blackness.[13] Latter-day Saints sometimes did just that—distanced themselves from their own Black brothers and sisters.

CHAPTER 5

LATTER-DAY SAINTS AND SLAVERY IN THE 1830S AND '40S

"Without reference to color or condition"

In the wake of the devastating expulsion from Jackson County in 1833, Latter-day Saint leaders spent the rest of the decade attempting to distance themselves from the abolitionist label. They issued statements and published news articles designed to shield Latter-day Saints who lived in the South or missionaries who preached there from similar backlashes like that aimed at W. W. Phelps and his fellow Saints in Jackson County.[1] By the time he was murdered, however, Joseph Smith's views on slavery had evolved to include a national plan for emancipation.

The Jackson County episode colored the Saints' view of national concerns over the immediate abolitionist movement then gaining ground in some locations. Rather than denounce slavery, the Latter-day Saints instead joined other denominations to distance themselves from immediate abolitionism. Methodists, Baptists, Catholics, Presbyterians, and even Quakers issued formal statements or spoke out against immediate abolitionism in the 1830s.[2]

In 1835, Latter-day Saint leaders followed suit. They issued a statement that honored the master-slave relationship and was intended to squelch fears that Latter-day Saints promoted slave revolts. "We do not believe it right to interfere with bond-servants neither preach the gospel to, nor baptize them contrary to the will and wish of their masters," they declared. It was not right, the statement continued, "to meddle with or influence [enslaved people] in the east, to cause them to be dissatisfied with their situations in this life, thereby jeopardizing the lives of men" (D&C 134:12). The decree was not issued as a revelation but rather called a "Declaration of Belief Regarding Governments and Laws in General." Leaders nonetheless included it in the Doctrine and Covenants.[3]

The appeasement to enslavers continued the following year, when Joseph Smith again spoke out on the issue. This time he sought to clarify his position on immediate abolitionism in a way that soothed Southern slaveholders and even drew on longstanding biblical rhetoric to justify slavery. Joseph Smith acknowledged that an antislavery sentiment seemed to dominate among his followers in the North. Latter-day Saints from the North "complain against their brethren of the same faith, who reside in the south," Smith noted. He worried that some Latter-day Saints "are ready to withdraw the hand of fellowship [from slaveholders in the South] because they will not renounce the principle of slavery and raise their voice against every thing of the kind."[4]

Joseph Smith urged "candid reflection" among his followers concerning the consequences of immediate abolitionism and even drew on the Bible to articulate a standard Christian defense of slavery, that God had cursed Canaan: "A servant of servants shall he be unto his brethren" (Genesis 9:25).[5] The curse of Noah or Ham, as it was sometimes called, was used among Christians, Jews, and Muslims as "the single greatest justification for Black slavery for more than a thousand years."[6] From a fraught interpretation of a few verses in the Bible, religious leaders of various denominations had long defended white people who enslaved Black people, and Joseph Smith now joined them. He admitted that he did not know "what could have been the design of the Almighty in this singular occurrence" but he was sure that "the curse is not yet taken off from the sons of Canaan." As a result, he cautioned that those who "interfere the least with the purposes of God in this matter, will come under the least condemnation before Him."[7]

Standard explanations at the time failed to clarify why Canaan, Ham's son, was "cursed" for Ham's supposed misdeed and why generations of people would be brutalized in slavery for an incident in which they took no part. What was it that Ham did that would lead to such dire consequences being meted out to his son and his son's supposed descendants? The entire episode violated the principle that Joseph Smith would later articulate as the second article of faith, that human beings are punished for their own sins and not for Adam's (or anyone else's) transgressions. In 1836, Smith nonetheless used the standard interpretation of those verses to imply God's sanction of slavery. Importantly, the supposed "curse" was slavery, not priesthood. In fact, Joseph Smith did not mention priesthood or make any such connection to ordination. He did make it clear that Latter-day Saints would not interfere with slavery.[8]

More succinctly, two years later, in response to the question "Are the Mormons abolitionists?," another Latter-day Saint newspaper, the *Elders' Journal*, published at Far West, Missouri, flatly declared "we do not believe in setting the Negroes free."[9] These were politically expedient stances designed to prevent a repeat of the Jackson County expulsion. Latter-day Saints understood what would happen if Missourians believed that they were opposed to slavery. Their survival as a community was at stake, and so they attempted to deflect the accusation that Latter-day Saints incited slave revolts. The statements were also meant to temper the growing chorus of voices among Joseph Smith's Northern followers who advocated for withdrawing fellowship from Southern slaveholders. Joseph Smith's position on slavery was also calculated to suppress opposition to Latter-day Saint missionaries then preaching in the South as well as to appease slaveholding Latter-day Saints and keep them in the fold.

Joseph Smith's views evolved, however, as the Saints abandoned Ohio and were driven from Missouri under a state-sanctioned extermination order. Anti-abolitionist violence diminished nationally at the same time that antislavery sentiments increased in Illinois, the Saints' new gathering place.[10]

Joseph Smith was thus freed from the earlier need to be overly sympathetic toward slavery but was nonetheless constrained by a desire to keep Southern converts in the fold. Even still he was now ready to "interfere" with the curse of Canaan and propose a national plan for emancipation.

By the time he was murdered at Carthage Jail in Hancock County, Illinois, Joseph Smith had arrived at a position of racial equality that rejected longstanding assumptions about the inherent inferiority of Black people. He also proposed a national plan to eradicate slavery based on government-funded emancipation, and he and other Latter-day Saint leaders openly acknowledged the discrepancy between the nation's founding ideals grounded in liberty and equality and the fact of slavery.[11]

In 1843, in a discussion at Springfield, Illinois, Smith expressed his most open ideas regarding racial equality: Black people were not biologically inferior but were impeded by a lack of educational opportunities and other environmental circumstances common to enslavement. "They come into the world slaves mentally & phy[s]ically. change their situation with the white & they would be like them," he argued. "They have souls & are subjects of salvation" he continued and even suggested that "Slaves in washington [were] more refined than the presidents."[12] Give them equal opportunity, in other words, and they could achieve equal or greater results.

Smith still did not favor race mixing, however, a point he made clear. "Had I any thing to do with the negro," he concluded, "I would confine them to by strict Laws to their own Species" but otherwise "put them on a national Equalization."[13] He did not specify at the time what he meant by "national equalization" but a sense of what he may have had in mind emerged the following year.

In 1844, Smith moved from a mere belief in equality toward an actual plan for national emancipation. Out of mounting frustration over the failure of national politicians to address the Saints' ongoing grievances over their expulsion from

Missouri and their corresponding loss of land, life, and property, Smith decided to run for president of the United States. His unlikely bid for the White House prompted him to put his ideas regarding slavery into a political plan grounded in compensated emancipation.[14]

Smith proposed to free enslaved people throughout the South, a process that he predicted could be complete by 1850. It was not immediate emancipation, but he did advocate for emancipation over the coming six years, a significantly accelerated pace of freedom in contrast to the existing gradual emancipation laws then in operation in some states, which dragged out the process for at least forty years.[15]

Smith's plan called on the federal government to compensate white enslavers for the loss of property such an emancipation would represent. He proposed to pay for the freedom of the enslaved through the sale of public lands and from a pay reduction leveled against members of Congress. "Break off the shackles from the poor Black man, and hire him to labor like other human beings," Joseph Smith insisted.[16]

Thus by the spring of 1844, Joseph Smith's prior biblical justification for slavery disappeared and was replaced by an expansive understanding of the interrelated nature of the entire human family. He now drew on the Bible as well as the founding documents of the United States to argue for universal human rights. He pointed to the great American paradox as a problem that needed resolution: a nation founded on the principles that "all men are created equal" simultaneously held "some two or three millions of people . . . as slaves for life, because the spirit in them is covered with a darker skin than ours."[17]

At least a part of the solution to that paradox came through an understanding of the broad commonality of the human family. Rather than looking to the book of Genesis and its curse of Canaan, this time Joseph Smith drew inspiration from the book of Acts to assert that "God has made of one

SLAVERY IN THE 1830S AND '40S

blood all nations of men for to dwell on the face of the earth" (see Acts 17:26).[18]

Smith thus came to view all people as members of the same human family. As a brother in that family who had experienced the violation of his rights, he asserted a platform grounded in racial equality. In his view, political officials "ought to be directed to ameliorate the condition of all, black or white, bond or free." He similarly called on the promises of the U.S. Constitution to be fulfilled and left no doubt that in his view that document "meant just what it said without reference to color or condition."[19]

In fact, Joseph Smith became so convinced that the U.S. Constitution failed to protect minority rights that he appointed a committee to draft a new constitution designed to rectify the problem. That constitution never came to fruition, but an early draft of it decried "cruelty, oppression, bondage, slavery, rapine, bloodshed, murder, carnage, desolation, and all the evils that blast the peace, exaltation, and glory of the universe." It declared that "God hath created all men free and equal" and repeated Smith's earlier claim that "one blood" united humankind.[20] It was a resounding endorsement of the equality and kinship of the entire human family.

Joseph Smith was murdered before he had an opportunity to put such ideals into practice. Up to this point, the Latter-day Saint lay leadership structure and its method of local control had worked to forestall questions over slavery that had split the nation's three largest Protestant denominations: the Methodists, Presbyterians, and Baptists. The Methodists, for example, questioned whether they should ordain white enslavers to leadership roles, and Baptists debated if enslavers should be allowed to serve as missionaries. When Northern members of those denominations adopted strict policies against such practices, adherents in the South broke off and started their own churches.[21]

In the 1830s and 1840s, Latter-day Saints avoided a similar fate. The Church's lay leadership structure meant that in the

South, white enslavers sometimes served as leaders and held the priesthood in branches that included their Black enslaved. Likewise in the North, men of various political persuasions, including abolitionists and those otherwise opposed to slavery, presided over local congregations, and Black men were ordained to the priesthood. As long as Latter-day Saints conformed to local laws and practices in the North and in the South, such a system worked. It may have even helped the Latter-day Saints to avoid the same type of conflict that split the Methodists, Baptists, and Presbyterians along a North/South divide.

Even still, this approach merely delayed the issue until Latter-day Saints gathered to what would become Utah Territory, a political entity without prior laws on slavery. Then the Saints would be forced to decide what to do about the issue and to write laws of their own making. No longer would Northern abolitionists and Southern enslavers, Black priesthood holders and Black enslaved people, continue to exist in the same Church as strangers and foreigners. After 1847 they would gather together in one location in a very mortal and politically messy household of faith.[22]

Even as antislavery sentiment grew stronger among Latter-day Saints in the North, missionaries continued to convert enslavers and their enslaved in the South. It was a tension that persisted in the Church until the Civil War and the Thirteenth Amendment to the U.S. Constitution finally eradicated slavery, but not until 1865. In the meantime, Latter-day Saint leaders tried to navigate the difficult challenges of creating a unified Church that welcomed free and enslaved Black people, abolitionists and anti-abolitionists, enslavers and those who found slavery abhorrent.

CHAPTER 6

UNIVERSALISM AT NAUVOO

"Persons of all languages, and of every tongue, and of every color"

In 1840, at Nauvoo, as the First Presidency contemplated the early success of missionaries gathering God's children from across the earth, they were unrestrained. "If the work roll forth with the same rapidity it has heretofore done, we may soon expect to see flocking to this place people from every land and from every nation, the polished European, the degraded Hottentot [a nineteenth-century term used to refer to Black tribal South Africans], and the shivering Laplander." They anticipated "persons of all languages, and of every tongue, and of every color; who shall with us worship the Lord of Hosts in his holy temple, and offer up their orisons in his sanctuary."[1] It was an indication that the First Presidency envisioned people "of every color" worshipping in the temple that they would start to build the following spring.

If Latter-day Saint leaders implemented racial restrictions following Joseph Smith's death, despite their announced intent to welcome people "of every color," there is no evidence of it. In 1845, Brigham Young sealed Lewis Dana, a Native American man from the Oneida tribe, to Mary Gont, a white woman, in the first known mixed-racial marriage of any type solemnized in a Latter-day Saint temple.[2] It was an indication of racial openness, but Native Americans were never barred from the priesthood, and Dana's conversion and temple experience were seen as evidence of the unfolding redemption of Native Americans, a positive sign rather than the negative terms with which Brigham Young would come to define race mixing between Black and white people.

Even still, there was at least one person of Black African ancestry who received temple rituals at Nauvoo in 1845. Sarah Ann Mode was born in Philadelphia in 1811 to Jesse Mode, who was Black, and Mary Shuell, who was white. Her father, Jesse, worked as the captain of a freighting ship stationed in Wilmington, Delaware, with a crew of all Black sailors. In 1848 he was arrested, imprisoned, and fined for violating a law that required at least one white man be on board a vessel manned by Black sailors.[3]

It is not clear if Sarah was aware of the plight of her father in 1848. By that point she was living far away in Winter Quarters among the Latter-day Saints. She had met and married a German-born immigrant named Peter Hofheintz back in Philadelphia, where the young couple first made their home. It was there that Sarah and Peter joined the Church in 1841. They worshiped in the Philadelphia branch until they migrated to Nauvoo the following year. Even though early census records described Sarah's family as free people of color, the 1840 and all subsequent census records described Sarah as white, an indication that she had likely passed as white by the time she arrived in Nauvoo.[4]

Sarah and Peter were devout Latter-day Saints. In 1843, Sarah was baptized as proxy in the font of the yet unfinished Nauvoo Temple in behalf of her brother Alexander, who presumably had died sometime before. In December 1844, she received her patriarchal blessing at the hands of John Smith, Joseph Smith's uncle. She was told her lineage came through the biblical prophet Joseph who was sold into Egypt. One year later Sarah and Peter received washing and anointing and endowment rituals at Nauvoo. They were later sealed to each other in 1855 in Brigham Young's office in Salt Lake City, a common location for such rituals at the time. Sarah lived the rest of her life in the Salt Lake Twelfth Ward, where she participated in Relief Society, made charitable contributions, and was rebaptized in 1879 as a show of her ongoing commitment to the Latter-day Saint cause.[5]

There is no indication that those who performed Sarah's temple and sealing rituals were aware of her mixed racial ancestry, but DNA studies among Sarah's descendants in the twenty-first century continue to reveal African ancestry. She is the earliest known person of Black African ancestry to receive complete temple rituals in the Church. The Latter-day Saint message really did draw people in from all branches of God's earthly family.

CHAPTER 7

RACE AT WINTER QUARTERS

"We [h]av[e] one of the best Elders"

After the Latter-day Saint expulsion from Nauvoo in 1846, one convert, William McCary, tested the boundaries of the Saints' inclusivity. McCary was a formerly enslaved man from Mississippi who worked as a musician and entertainer before he arrived in Nauvoo in late 1845. He converted to the Church early the next year and married Lucy Stanton, a white Latter-day Saint who had previously joined the Church as a teenager in the Kirtland region. McCary sometimes claimed to be of Native American ancestry rather than African American, an assertion that was likely calculated to place him higher on America's racial ladder than acknowledging his status as formerly enslaved might.[1] Regardless of his claims, not all Latter-day Saints were convinced. Wilford Woodruff noted that McCary "professed to be an Indian" but most Saints "believed him to be a descendant of Ham."[2]

McCary sometimes made claims to prophetic authority and spiritual power, which drew suspicion from some Latter-day Saints and devotion from others. Latter-day Saints at Winter Quarters variously referred to him as "a half blooded Indian,"[3] "the Coolurd man,"[4] "the Indian prophet,"[5] "a half breed Indian negro,"[6] "the negro prophet,"[7] "a mulatto or querterrun,"[8] and "the Indian musician."[9]

On March 26, 1847, McCary sought an audience with Brigham Young and other Church leaders to address his treatment at the hands of fellow members of the Church but also to share his prophetic claims. The resulting interview is a singular event in Latter-day Saint history. McCary and his wife Lucy Stanton appeared before eight Latter-day Saint Apostles, including Brigham Young, who led the Church at the time as President of the Quorum of the Twelve. The interview was wide-ranging and covered issues of race, identity, and prophetic claims.

McCary complained that he was "hypocritically abused" among the Latter-day Saints and had experienced racism. When McCary and his wife passed by, some people in camp scornfully made reference to the interracial couple. In response, McCary asserted a Native American identity for himself. "I came in as a red man," he said, and "want to go out as a red man." He remained grateful for his baptism, but nonetheless struggled with his lack of acceptance among the Saints.[10]

Brigham Young answered with an appeal to the New Testament and the broad commonality among all of God's children. Paraphrasing Acts 17:26, Young said, "Its nothing to do with the blood, for of one blood has God made all flesh." In an effort to calm McCary's worries, Young reinforced the commonality of the entire human family. Not only did God create racial diversity out of "one blood"; Young insisted that Latter-day Saints did not discriminate even in distributing priesthood authority. He then cited Q. Walker Lewis in the Lowell, Massachusetts, branch as his proof: "We [h]av[e] one of the best Elders[,] an African in Lowell—a barber," he told McCary. Even Black men were welcome and eligible for the priesthood, Young affirmed. McCary declared himself "satisfied" with such an answer and announced that "if any one molests me I will come to bro. Brigham."[11]

The interview continued in somewhat arbitrary directions after that but eventually returned to McCary's standing among the Saints. "I am not a Pres[iden]t, or a leader of the p[eo]pl[e]," McCary lamented, but merely a "common bro[the]r," something he attributed to the fact that he was "a little shade darker." Brigham Young again asserted a universal ideal and told McCary, "We don't care about the color." McCary liked hearing that from Brigham Young but still wondered if the other apostles shared the same sentiments. "Do I hear that from all?" he asked. Those present responded with a unified "aye." Brigham Young counseled McCary to ignore "what the p[eo]pl[e] say, shew by your actions that you don't care for what they say—all we do is to serve the Lord with all our hearts," he insisted. McCary said he was willing to "pick up the cross of Christ," and the meeting ended.[12]

It was a remarkable exchange on several counts, but none more important than the fact that it reinforced the Saints' global vision to gather all of God's children into the gospel fold. It took place in March 1847, almost three years after Joseph Smith's murder, and demonstrated an ongoing commitment to the broader relatedness of the entire human family. Significantly, it put Brigham Young on record as favorably aware of Q. Walker Lewis as a Black priesthood holder. Young called Lewis "one of the best Elders" and specified that he understood him to be of "African" descent. Brigham Young also declared, "We don't care about the color." It was a striking example of Latter-day Saint universalist sentiment and a stark contrast to the position Brigham Young would adopt less than five years later.

CHAPTER 8

OLD TESTAMENT CURSES AND THE BOOK OF ABRAHAM

"Cursed as regards the Priesthood"

After Brigham Young's interview with William McCary, he would lead a group of Latter-day Saint pioneers into the Salt Lake Valley and then return to Winter Quarters by the fall of 1847. In Young's absence, McCary moved across the Missouri River to Mosquito Creek and attracted followers to join him in his own religious movement. Elder Parely P. Pratt, who was not present for the March meeting, spoke out against McCary by the end of April, and in doing so he described a racial priesthood curse.

Pratt was upset over the ongoing splintering of Saints who followed after competing religious leaders in the wake of Joseph Smith's death. "Ye who want to scatter[,] go and scatter to the 4 winds," Pratt challenged, "for the Lord can do without you and the church can do without you[,] for we want the pure in heart to go with us over the mountains." Pratt specifically called out James Strang, one leader of a schismatic group, and William McCary, another person he considered a detractor. "If people want to follow Strang," Pratt said, that was up to them. If they want "to follow this Black man who has got the blood of Ham in him which linege [*sic*] was cursed as regards the Priesthood," that was also their choice, but Pratt disapproved.[1]

In this instance, Pratt seemed to paraphrase the book of Abraham as the source for his idea, a text that Joseph Smith produced and that was first published in 1842 in the *Times and Seasons* newspaper at Nauvoo.[2] Even though there is no contemporary evidence that Smith interpreted the verses in

Abraham to validate a racial priesthood restriction, Church leaders after him did draw on it for justification.

The book speaks of a "king of Egypt" who was a "descendant from the loins of Ham, and was a partaker of the blood of the Canaanites by birth." It goes on to describe a daughter of Ham, a woman named Egyptus, whose son became a pharaoh. The pharaoh was "righteous" in that he established his kingdom based on wise and just principles, but he participated in idol worship and human sacrifice (see Abraham 1:5–11). He tried to "imitate" priesthood with idol worship. He was also not the firstborn son of a presiding patriarch, but was the son of Egyptus, a matriarch (see Abraham 1:21–27).

Joseph Smith established patriarchal descent for the position of presiding patriarch as the Restoration began and seemed to have an Old Testament model in mind when he did so. He used the language of "the right of Priesthood" when he ordained his father to that position, and following his father's death he ordained his oldest surviving brother, Hyrum Smith, to the same office.[3]

In the book of Abraham example, however, the pharaoh violated patriarchal descent. As the book of Abraham explained, pharaoh was "of that lineage by which he could not have the right of Priesthood" even though he attempted to claim it through Noah. He was thus "cursed . . . as pertaining to the Priesthood" (Abraham 1:21–27). The book of Abraham portrays the problem in part as matriarchal descent but suggests that the real issue was the pharaoh's idol worship. Patriarchal descent on its own would not have guaranteed the pharaoh the priesthood, but repentance might have. Abraham abandoned the idol worship of his fathers and desired to "keep the commandments of God," which made him "a rightful heir, a High Priest, holding the right belonging to the fathers" (Abraham 1:2). Repentance made Abraham eligible for the priesthood, not lineage. Leaders like Pratt, who were immersed in a fraught nineteenth-century racial culture, however, understood the problem racially instead.[4]

OLD TESTAMENT CURSES

In doing so they used the phrase from the book of Abraham, "cursed . . . as pertaining to the Priesthood," or in Pratt's words, "cursed as regards the Priesthood," as shorthand language to justify a racial restriction. Brigham Young, however, did not use the same phrase, and as we will learn, he would draw only on Cain's murder of Abel as his explanation. The book of Abraham, in fact, was not canonized in Young's lifetime. Latter-day Saint leaders added it to the scriptural canon in 1880, three years after Young's death. It nonetheless offered ready justification for the racial restriction, both before and after its canonization.[5]

The use of supposed racial curses, whether from the Bible, book of Abraham, or Book of Mormon, were grounded in misunderstandings of what curses actually meant to the people who wrote them into scripture. Curses existed as a human or divine expression in scripture, a way to wish for judgment, punishment, or misfortune on someone or even an entire group of people. They also existed as a part of a covenant pattern in ancient times. The children of Israel in the Old Testament, for example, would have been familiar with an ancient covenant pattern that structures the book of Deuteronomy. Lehi follows the same model in the Book of Mormon.[6]

The pattern involved leaders reminding God's covenant people of the things God had done for them, promising them blessings if they kept their covenants, and warning them of curses if they broke their covenants. This pattern played out in both the Book of Mormon and Deuteronomy:

- Lehi told his followers "many things" and "rehearsed unto them how great things the Lord had done for them in bringing them out of the land of Jerusalem" (2 Nephi 1:1–4).
- In Deuteronomy, the Lord similarly declares to the children of Israel, "I am the Lord thy God, which brought thee out of the land of Egypt, from the house of bondage" (Deuteronomy 5:6).

Next, God pledges to bless His followers who keep their promises to Him:

- "All these blessing shall come on thee, and overtake thee, if thou shalt hearken unto the voice of the Lord thy God," the book of Deuteronomy declares as it lists a variety of blessings promised to the faithful (Deuteronomy 28:1–14).
- Likewise, Lehi tells his followers that inasmuch as they shall keep God's commandments they "shall prosper in the land" (2 Nephi 1:20).

The final part of the pattern involved consequences for breaking one's covenants. In the language of the Old Testament, a consequence was a curse.

- Lehi tells his followers that if they broke their promises to God "cursed shall be the land" and "a cursing should come upon you for the space of many generations; and ye are visited by sword, and by famine" (2 Nephi 1:7, 18).
- Deuteronomy likewise explains: "I set before you this day a blessing and a curse; a blessing, if ye obey the commandments of the Lord your God, which I command you this day: and a curse, if ye will not obey the commandments of the Lord your God, but turn aside out of the way which I command you this day" (Deuteronomy 11:26–28).

As the children of Israel viewed it, a covenantal curse was a divine consequence for sin. In the covenant context, the curse was overcome through repentance and was not multigenerational (unless multiple generations refused to repent).

Outside of the covenantal context, people in the Old Testament sometimes ascribed curses to their enemies and sometimes used curses to distinguish between those in favor with God and those who they believed fell outside of God's favor. The curses of Cain and Ham are two notable examples. The Old Testament uses "curses" in both experiences to signal that Ham and Cain had violated accepted norms. Those who recorded those stories believed that there were corresponding curses associated with the violations. Importantly, however, neither curse was racial, and in Joseph Smith's version of the Cain story, repentance nullified the curse: God warned Cain that there was a "cursing which I will put upon thee, except thou repent," and when he did not repent he was "cursed from the earth" (Moses 5:25, 36). That simply meant that when Cain tilled the ground "it shall not henceforth yield unto thee her strength" (Moses 5:37). There was nothing racial about the curse of Cain, and the same was true for the curse of Ham.

Yet, those who read those two Old Testament curses in the eighteenth and nineteenth centuries sometimes added their own interpretations to them and turned them into racial curses designed to justify discrimination in their day. In a fraught nineteenth-century American racial context, Latter-day Saints inherited longstanding scriptural interpretations that fell into this pattern. By the time Joseph Smith established the Church in 1830, the standard Christian interpretations of the curses of Cain and Ham were racial. It was therefore natural for Latter-day Saints to apply similar understandings to two curses in their own scriptures, one in the book of Abraham (see Abraham 1:21–27) and the other in the Book of Mormon (see 2 Nephi 5:21).

As with the book of Abraham, repentance in the Book of Mormon nullified the curse. Speaking of the Lamanites, the Lord said, "I will cause that they shall be loathsome unto thy people, *save they shall repent* of their iniquities" (2 Nephi 5:22; emphasis added). True to His word, when the Lamanites repented, they were welcomed into a covenant relationship with God (see Helaman 13:1). Their relationship with God, in other words, was not based on the color of their skin, but on their devotion to Him and His commandments.

Light and dark are used metaphorically throughout scripture to indicate good and bad, righteousness and wickedness.[7] It is a colorized binary that lent itself to a racialized understanding of scripture and a racialized understanding of who Black people are in God's family.[8] If anything, such explanations brought the sin of racism into the nineteenth-century Church, a sin that did become multigenerational as it entrenched itself among Latter-day Saints. Like all curses, however, it is one that repentance can overcome.

Dark skin is not a curse. God does not afflict people with blackness as a consequence for sin. In fact, in 2013, the First Presidency and Quorum of the Twelve Apostles disavowed any notion "that black skin is a sign of divine disfavor or curse."[9] As the prophet Jacob warned in the Book of Mormon, such thinking can lead us to persecute others "because ye suppose that ye are better than they" (Jacob 2:13). He reminded the Nephites that God "created all flesh" and that "one being is as precious in his sight as the other" (Jacob 2:21).

Jacob warned the Nephites that unless they repented of their pride and feelings of superiority that the Lamanites' "skins will be whiter than yours, when ye shall be brought with them before the throne of God" (Jacob 3:8). It is a fitting metaphor designed to combat racism. God does not judge us based on skin color, but He does judge us based on how we treat each other according to the color of our skin. If we engage in racism, Jacob warns, those we "revile" will be purer than we are on Judgment Day.

Pratt's flawed understanding notwithstanding, his reference to a cursed priesthood did not establish a new precedent or play out in any practical way, even in regard to William McCary. Pratt suggested that McCary was "cursed" in an attempt to discredit him and stem the flow of his followers out of the Church. Future leaders did not refer back to Pratt or remember his statement as a pattern for Church policy. It nonetheless indicated that at least one Apostle, as early as 1847, drew on the book of Abraham as a source for a priesthood curse.[10]

As for William McCary, he continued to attract a following until his worship practices came to light. One local leader, Nelson Whipple, eventually learned of McCary's activities.

"He was in favor of holding his meetings of the men and women separately, saying that his teaching to the men and to the women was entirely different," Whipple explained. According to Whipple, McCary "had a number of women sealed to him" in a sexualized ceremony of his own invention. When news of McCary's exploits reached leaders at Winter Quarters, they excommunicated McCary and his followers.[11]

McCary's interview with Brigham Young and other Apostles in March 1847 marked a transition in racial openness in the Church. Perhaps in response to news of McCary's sexual exploits with white women and a report of another interracial couple who were also members of the Church, Brigham Young would begin moving in a decidedly different direction on matters of race.

PHASE TWO

SEGREGATED PRIESTHOOD AND TEMPLES

CHAPTER 9

LATTER-DAY SAINTS AND THE FEAR OF RACE MIXING

"I wish to know if this is the order of God or tolerated in this Church"

At the same time that Brigham Young led the vanguard pioneers into the Salt Lake Valley in the summer of 1847, he sent a man by the name of William I. Appleby to survey the conditions of the various branches of the Church along the east coast of the United States. Appleby was a convert from New Jersey, baptized seven years earlier, and a dedicated missionary.[1] By his own account, he traveled nearly 2,000 miles that summer, going from branch to branch "counselling, instructing, organizing, adjusting difficulties, and getting things in order."[2]

When Appleby arrived at Lowell, Massachusetts, what he found there disturbed him. In a letter to Brigham Young, Appleby expressed his concern: "At this place I found a coloured brother, by name of 'Lewis,' a barber, an Elder in the Church, ordained some years ago by Wm Smith," he wrote. In doing so, Appleby was not telling Brigham Young anything that he did not already know. Young himself had called Q. Walker Lewis "one of the best Elders" and noted that he was "an African" less than three months earlier at Winter Quarters.[3] As events continued to unfold, however, Brigham Young's interactions with Appleby further influenced his shift in thinking on racial matters.

Appleby learned that Lewis had a son named Enoch "who is married to a white girl, and both members of the Church." Appleby then expressed his concern to Brigham Young about both Walker Lewis's ordination to the priesthood as well as his son Enoch's marriage to Mary Matilda Webster, a white Latter-day Saint also in the Lowell branch. "Now dear Br[other]," he wrote, "I wish to know if this is the order of God or tolerated in this Church," that is, "to ordain Negroes to the Priesthood, and allow amalgamation. If it is I desire to know it, as I have yet got to learn it," Appleby prodded.[4]

Appleby was less reserved in his journal than he was in his letter to Brigham Young, especially after he met Enoch Lewis and Mary Webster in person. After his visit to their home he wrote in his journal that "in looking for a Br[other] in the Church, I called at a House,—a coloured man resided there; I set myself down for a few moments, presently in came quite a good looking White Woman, about 22 years old I should think, with blushing cheeks, and was introduced to me as the negro's wife, an infant in a cradle near by bore evidence of the fact." In recounting his visit, Appleby could hardly contain himself, "Oh! Woman, thought I, where is thy shame . . . Respect for thy family, thyself—for thy offspring and above all the law of God?" Even more upsetting for Appleby was the fact that Enoch and Mary were Latter-day Saints, "for indeed I felt ashamed and not only ashamed, but disgusted, when I was informed they were both members of o[ur] Church!"[5]

In Appleby's estimation, interracial marriage violated "the law of God," a common perspective of the time. In many states such marriages also violated civil laws. By the 1820s, seventeen out of twenty-three states in the United States had banned marriage between Black and white people, and by the outbreak of the Civil War in 1861, twenty-eight out of thirty-four states did so. Massachusetts, the state where Enoch Lewis and Mary Webster lived, was not among them, however. Enoch and Mary's marriage was legal, but that did not mean that it was socially acceptable.[6]

Joseph Smith at Nauvoo had prevented two Black men from marrying white women. With no explanation for the distinction, he fined one man twenty-five dollars and the other five dollars. In his capacity as judge in Nauvoo, Joseph

Smith was enforcing an Illinois state law that barred interracial marriage. The punishment he imposed was significantly less than the law mandated, possibly because the men intended to marry white women but had not yet done so.[7] For Brigham Young, however, the concern stretched beyond law to theology and would shape his views regarding priesthood ordination.

It is not clear when Brigham Young received Appleby's summer letter, but the two men met in person at Winter Quarters on December 3, 1847. Young had returned from his initial foray to the Great Basin, and Appleby had also arrived and was anxious to give his report. Young and a majority of the Apostles met with Appleby to learn of his trip and to hear of conditions among the various branches of the Church in the East. The meeting began at six thirty in the evening and did not break up until ten thirty, when Heber C. Kimball "retired to bed," leaving Brigham Young, Orson Hyde, and Willard Richards "chatting until one oclock." Despite such a lengthy discussion, the official notes of the meeting captured less than thirteen handwritten lines. Most of those notes deal with concern over race mixing and offer only a glimpse into the thoughts of those present.[8]

Appleby informed the Apostles that "Wm Smith ordained a Black man Elder at Lowell & he has married a White girl & they have a child." Appleby, or notetaker Thomas Bullock, seemed to confuse Walker Lewis, who Apostle William Smith had ordained to the priesthood, with his son Enoch Lewis, who married Mary Webster. In any case, the concern was interracial marriage, or "amalgamation" in the language of the day, and Appleby felt it important enough to bring before the Latter-day Saint Apostles.[9]

Brigham Young's response was stern and severe, even in the context of the times: "If they [Enoch and Mary] were far away from the Gentiles," he insisted, "they wo[u]ld all [h]av[e] to be killed—when they mingle seed it is death to all."[10] Some states had stipulated the death penalty as punishment for Black men who raped white women, but Brigham

Young spoke of marriage, not rape. In this particular case, he made the statement to an intimate gathering of Apostles and William Appleby, but he would return to the same position in more public settings in Utah Territory. In 1852, for instance, he again spoke out against race mixing to the Utah territorial legislature, and then in 1863 in a public sermon delivered at the Tabernacle in Salt Lake City, he proclaimed that "if the white man who belongs to the chosen seed mixes his blood with the seed of Cain, the penalty, under the law of God, is death on the spot."[11] In making such statements, Brigham Young spoke, as he sometimes did, with extreme hyperbole. He even admitted as much in 1848 when he acknowledged, "I frequently sa[y] 'cut his infernal throat'; I dont mean any such thing."[12] Brigham Young's stance was never encoded into Utah law, but it did likely shape attitudes among Latter-day Saints regarding violence, interracial marriage, and the status of Black people in general.[13]

At Winter Quarters, Brigham Young next explored a hypothetical scenario, perhaps in response to Appleby, who likely remained "disgusted" that Enoch Lewis and Mary Webster were members of the Church. "If a black man & white woman come to you & demand baptism can you deny them?" Brigham Young asked. "The law is their seed shall not be amalgamated," he answered. "Mulattoes r like mules[,] they cant have the children, but if they will be Eunuchs for the Kingdom of ~~Gods~~ Heaven's sake they may have a place in the Temple."[14]

Apostle Orson Hyde agreed with Brigham Young and insisted that "if girls marry the half breeds they r throwing themselves away & becoming as one of them," which Brigham Young said was "wrong for them to do."[15] Hyde and Brigham Young suggested that people of mixed racial descent, or "mulattoes," could be baptized and even "have a place in the Temple," but they would need to be "Eunuchs for the Kingdom of . . . Heaven's sake."[16] Young here seems to reference the idea then in circulation that race mixing created sterility in the offspring of interracial couples.

Dr. Josiah Clark Nott, a noted American anthropologist, had popularized such views. Nott was firmly against amalgamation, the offspring of whom he referred to as "hybrids." In 1843, he published an influential article titled "The Mulatto a Hybrid—Probable Extermination of the Two Races if the Whites and Blacks are Allowed to Intermarry." Nott proposed a hypothetical scenario in which "a hundred white men and one hundred black women were put together on an Island, and cut off from all intercourse with the rest of the world." In such circumstances, Nott predicted the island's inhabitants "would in time become extinct." In his estimation, "the mulatto is a degenerate, unnatural offspring, doomed by nature to work out its own destruction."[17]

It is impossible to know if Brigham Young, Orson Hyde, or William Appleby read Nott or were otherwise influenced by him, but their views meshed with Nott's. At the very least, Hyde, Young, and Appleby demonstrated an awareness of certain ideas about race then circulating in American society. They introduced them into this discussion at Winter Quarters, where they influenced racial thinking within the faith over the course of the rest of the nineteenth century.

Even still, the discussion centered on race mixing, not priesthood. In fact, the sparse surviving minutes do not mention a priesthood ban or curse. If those gathered on December 3, 1847, discussed a racial priesthood restriction, Thomas Bullock failed to capture it in his notes.[18] Appleby's own journal entry for that meeting is equally silent on the matter.[19] It would be five more years before Brigham Young would openly articulate a racial priesthood restriction, and he would do so in a debate with Apostle Orson Pratt before the territorial legislature.[20] His concern over race mixing, nonetheless, informed his decision on priesthood and helps to account for his shift in position.

CHAPTER 10

BRIGHAM YOUNG OPENLY ARTICULATES A RACIAL RESTRICTION

"I know they can't bear rule in [the] Priesthood"

An 1851 census counted forty-six enslaved African American men and women in Utah Territory, spread between Davis, Utah, and Salt Lake Counties.[1] It was an undercount of enslaved people, but that year some enslavers took their enslaved to San Bernardino, California, so that somewhere between thirty and forty enslaved African Americans lived in Utah Territory when the legislature met in early 1852. That number would remain fairly stable over the next decade.[2]

Up to 1852, Latter-day Saint leaders had adopted a policy of neutrality regarding both Indigenous and African American slavery in the territory. It existed by custom, but there were no laws on the books to govern it. Influential friend and advisor to the Saints, Thomas L. Kane, himself an outspoken critic of slavery, had counseled Brigham Young and Latter-day Saint leaders to avoid taking a stance on the issue, especially if the Saints hoped to be taken seriously in their bid to gain statehood.[3] Kane admonished that it "will not do for you to take the slavery question or Antislavery or any other side but the nutral [*sic*]."[4]

In 1852, however, lawmakers met to decide what laws should govern the relationship between white enslavers and Black enslaved people as well as to address Indigenous slavery in the territory. Following sometimes heated debate, the legislature passed An Act for the Relief of Indian Slaves and Prisoners and An Act in Relation to Service. The first law legalized the purchasing of Native American children and indenturing them as apprentices for not more than twenty years.

BRIGHAM YOUNG ARTICULATES RACIAL RESTRICTION

The second law defined Black slaves as servants and granted them some rights not accorded under chattel slave laws in the South, including a requirement to educate enslaved people and to defer to their consent if they were to be sold to another master or taken from the territory. It nonetheless allowed for those brought to the territory as enslaved people to be held in servitude for life. Children born to enslaved parents in Utah Territory, however, did not inherit their parents' condition, making it a conservative form of gradual emancipation.[5]

Brigham Young and Orson Pratt did not see eye to eye on the two laws. Pratt believed both bills amounted to slavery, and he wanted them rejected. Lawmakers also debated Utah's election bill, and Pratt advocated for Black male voting rights in the territory. In contrast, Brigham Young argued that Black people bore the weight of biblical curses and were inferior to white people. He mixed his views on race and slavery with his views on priesthood and articulated a racial priesthood restriction.

It is evident from surviving sources that lawmakers did not learn of the racial restriction for the first time at the legislative session. Brigham Young, nonetheless, first publicly articulated the restriction in two key speeches to lawmakers. In addition, the legislative session marked a transition among Latter-day Saint leaders in terms of their willingness to openly talk about it. Within three months of the lawmaking session, Willard Richards, counselor to Brigham Young in the First Presidency, spoke of the ban in a newspaper article published in the *Deseret News*.[6] Four other Latter-day Saint–owned newspapers followed suit over the next five years.[7]

As early as 1849, in a private meeting with Church leaders, Brigham Young laid out his rationale for the racial restriction. Newly ordained Apostle Lorenzo Snow "presented the case of the African Race for a chance of redemption & unlock the door to them." There is no indication what "case" Snow made. The brief notes of the 1849 meeting only indicate that Brigham Young responded to Snow's presentation by establishing the basic argument that he would more fully express to the territorial legislature three years later.[8]

Brigham Young viewed the entire human family as a vast network of connections from the premortal realm, a great ordered chain of belonging. One task of mortality was to re-create the premortal network and seal human beings into the structured order of heaven.[9] In Young's estimation, however, when Cain murdered his brother Abel, Cain disrupted that order. As he explained in 1849, the "curse remains on them [Black people] bec[ause] Cain cut off the lives of Abel to hedge up his way & take the lead but the L[or]d has given them blackness, so as to give the children of Abel an opportunity to keep his place with his desc[endant]s in the et[erna]l worlds."[10] Cain tried to usurp Abel's position and eliminate Abel's posterity. As Brigham Young explained it, the consequence was a racial curse that supposedly marked Cain with black skin and cursed him and his presumed descendants from the priesthood.

Brigham Young stuck with this explanation and expanded on it at the 1852 legislative session. On January 23, after Elder George A. Smith introduced An Act in Relation to Service to the legislature, Young responded with a speech that described a priesthood curse: "The Lord God said that cursed [be] old Cain and [God] said that [only after] the last drop of [the] blood of Abel receives the priesthood and enjoys the blessings [of it], then Cain is calculated to have his share [but] not until then," he explained. "Consequently I am firm in [my] belief of servitude."[11]

Apostle and legislator Orson Pratt stridently disagreed with Brigham Young and argued against slavery and multigenerational curses. Four days after Brigham Young spoke, Pratt weighed in on the proposed legislation and moved that "the bill be rejected in-toto." He then gave an impassioned speech in defense of his position. He called slavery "a great evil" and was dismayed that his fellow legislators would consider legalizing slavery where prior laws did not already sanction it. "Shall we introduce this evil in our midst? No! I hope [there is] wisdom, light, and intelligence enough within the bosoms of this honorable council to spurn the idea [with] indignation," Pratt insisted.[12]

He argued that only God could administer curses and that they were specific to a given time and place. In his estimation, enslavers who suggested that biblical curses were still in force had taken it upon themselves "to execute the curse of Almighty upon that race without being commanded to do it and they will have to be punished for rising up and inflicting this curse upon [the] descendants of Adam." Even if God did curse Ham or Canaan or Cain in the Bible, Pratt did not believe that such curses passed down to anyone else. He rejected the notion that nineteenth-century enslavers, including Latter-day Saints, had any authority from God to enslave Black people. "Shall we assume the right without the voice of [the] Lord speaking to us and commanding us to [introduce] slavery into our territory?" Pratt queried. He was dismayed by such a prospect.[13]

Pratt also feared the consequences for Latter-day Saint missionary work in foreign countries if legislators legalized slavery in Utah Territory. Slavery was on its way out across the globe; how could Latter-day Saints introduce it in Utah? he wondered. "[When] in [our] situation we are legislating in [the] capacity of people who desire to serve God, in [the] capacity [to] be the most benefit to [the] nations abroad, is it not known to this honorable council the light in which slavery is looked upon by almost every enlightened nation or heathen?" Pratt questioned. "They look upon it with disgust," he answered.[14]

People of African descent were not guilty of some premortal sin for which slavery was the penalty, Pratt said. "Shall we take then the innocent African that has committed no sin and damn him to slavery and bondage without receiving any authority from heaven to do [so]? That they and their children shall be servants to us and our children? The idea is preposterous in my mind," he demanded. "For us to bind the African because he is different from us in color [is] enough to cause the angels in heaven to blush! Let me make my [conscience to] be clear from this," Pratt pleaded.[15]

It was a remarkable speech that denounced longstanding justifications for slavery that predated the founding of the Church. Brigham Young bought into those justifications while Pratt rejected them. In sum, the two men did not see eye to eye on Utah's proposed bill.[16]

Pratt's disagreement with Brigham Young, however, was still not over. Both men spoke again on February 4, the same day that Brigham Young signed An Act in Relation to Service into law, but Pratt's speech was unfortunately not recorded. Legislators passed an "Act in Relation to Elections" that day, a law which stipulated that white men over twenty-one could vote in the territory, a typical standard for voting across the nation, with only a few New England states at the time allowing Black men to vote on par with white men. Even though Pratt's speech does not survive, fellow legislator Hosea Stout said that Pratt voted against "all acts prohibiting the right of Negroes the privileges of voting."[17] Brigham Young also implied that Pratt made vocal objections to the election bill. In fact, Young indicated a brewing disagreement when he claimed that Pratt's actions that day were designed to "stick his thumb into me."[18] Young's speech the following day thus appears structured as an answer to Pratt's advocacy for Black male voting rights.

On February 5, Brigham Young rejected Black voting rights at the same time that he reasserted a racial priesthood restriction and argued that white people were superior to Black people. It represents Brigham Young's most complete and forceful articulation of a priesthood restriction. There is no record in which Brigham Young mentions a revelation authorizing the restriction. Instead, he relied primarily on his interpretation of the biblical "Curse of Cain" at the same time that he directly challenged Pratt's contention that African American men should be allowed to vote.

Brigham Young declared: "If there never was a prophet or apostle of Jesus Christ [who] spoke it before, I tell you, this people that are commonly called Negroes are [the] children of Cain. I know they are; I know they can't bear rule in [the] Priesthood, [in the] first sense of [the] word."[19] Brigham Young also asserted, "in [the] Kingdom of God on earth, a man who has the African blood in him can't hold one jot nor tittle of Priesthood."[20]

Here Brigham Young openly acknowledged that he was striking out on his own in declaring a priesthood restriction. He told legislators that even if "there never was a prophet or apostle of Jesus Christ [who] spoke it before," he was saying it now. He thus claimed to be the first prophet to say it. He did not evoke Joseph Smith as the source for the priesthood restriction or for his understanding of the curse of Cain. He did not claim a revelation from God as his source either. He said instead, "I tell you."[21]

Orson Pratt may have denied a connection between Cain and Black people in his speech the day before, prompting Brigham Young's assertion. In another strident antislavery speech, this time delivered in 1856, Pratt declared: "We have no proof that the Africans are the descendants of old Cain who was cursed, and even if we had that evidence we have not been ordered to inflict that [curse] upon that race."[22] It was the only rationale which Brigham Young offered for the priesthood restriction, and Pratt rejected it.

Furthermore, Brigham Young did not explain how it was that Black people were now cursed from the priesthood in 1852, when five years earlier he had favorably acknowledged a Black priesthood holder. In his interview with William McCary at Winter Quarters, Young had called Q. Walker Lewis "one of the best Elders, an African." Young failed to reconcile his reversal or to explain how it was that a Black priesthood holder could go from being "one of the best Elders" in 1847 to being "cursed" from the priesthood by 1852.[23]

Fear of race mixing likely played the most significant role in Brigham Young's reversal. Race mixing concerned him ever since he learned of William McCary's schismatic group and

Enoch Lewis's mixed-racial marriage in 1847, and he saved some of his most pointed comments for that very topic in his speech to the legislature. In barring Black men from priesthood ordination, Brigham Young in essence barred them from temple admission, because ordination accompanied temple rituals. In practice, it meant that he would not have to deal with interracial temple marriages.

Brigham Young imagined a hypothetical scenario wherein the entire leadership of the Church declared it right to "mingle" their seed with the seed of Cain and thereby embrace the "abolition doctrines." On "that [very] day and hour the priesthood [would be] taken from this church and kingdom [and] God leaves us [to our fate]," Young proclaimed. It was a dire prediction that Young then punctuated with force. The moment "we consent to take the seed of Cain, the church [must] go to destructions," he said. Race mixing would spell an end to the priesthood, he claimed, and to the entire Church.[24]

Young then related the priesthood restriction to voting rights. "I will not consent for a moment to have the children of Cain rule me, nor my brethren, when it is not right," he explained. "If they cannot bear rule in [the] church of God, what business have they in bearing rule in [the] state and government affairs of [this] territory?"[25] Brigham Young thus reasoned that the curse of Cain denied people of African descent a right to the priesthood and then argued that if they could not officiate in God's Church, they should also be denied the right to participate in civil government or even vote.

"You cannot find within men upon [the] earth [who are of the] seed of Cain [any] that [possess] knowledge and sensibility [enough to vote]," Brigham Young maintained. "Not one of [the] children of old Cain has any right to bear rule in government affairs from first to last; [they have] no business there," he insisted.[26] "[We] just [as well] make [a] bill here for mules to vote as Negroes [and] Indians," he declared. Underlying Brigham Young's sentiments was opposition to racial equality.

"What we are trying to do today [is] to make [the] Negro equal with us in all our privileges," he said. "My voice shall be against [it] all the day long."[27]

Despite Brigham Young's strident stance against Black voting rights, Orson Pratt remained unconvinced. If Pratt was allowed to respond to Brigham Young's speech, legislative minutes fail to specify. Yet Pratt did answer Brigham Young with two votes on the afternoon of February 5. Lawmakers passed the Cedar City and Fillmore, Utah, incorporation bills that day, two laws that were typically rubber-stamped by lawmakers, yet Pratt voted against both bills. Legislative minutes indicate that he did so "on the ground that colored people were there prohibited from voting."[28] Pratt stuck to his convictions and was willing to stand alone for racial equality.

CHAPTER 11

ORSON PRATT AND A PREMORTAL EXPLANATION

"Others receive bodies among the African negroes"

There is no indication that Elder Orson Pratt ever did accept Brigham Young's rationale for a priesthood restriction. In fact, the debate between the two men seemed to continue at least to the 1860s. In 1853, Pratt offered his own explanation for a priesthood restriction, this time drawing on the book of Abraham and the premortal existence for inspiration. Brigham Young and Orson Pratt, thus, articulated the two competing ideas for the racial restrictions that continued to exist in tension with each other until officially disavowed by the First Presidency and Quorum of the Twelve Apostles in 2013.[1]

The central problem in Brigham Young's justification for withholding the priesthood from people of Black African descent was that it violated a fundamental gospel principle articulated in the second article of faith. Joseph Smith rejected the longstanding idea that human beings were born into original sin and that because Adam fell his descendants inherited his transgression. Instead, Joseph Smith taught that each person would be "punished for their own sins, and not for Adam's transgression."[2]

Brigham Young's priesthood curse, however, held the supposed descendants of Cain responsible for a murder in which they took no part. It was a reversion back to a version of original sin, but only for Black people, and it violated the second article of faith. Perhaps to get around this theological conundrum, Orson Pratt, in 1853, posited his own justification for a racial priesthood restriction.

ORSON PRATT AND A PREMORTAL EXPLANATION

Pratt weighed in on the matter in an article in *The Seer*, a New York City–based newspaper he edited. His explanation honored the principle of agency and avoided divine curses. Pratt did not mention the priesthood restriction in the 1852 legislative session, although he clearly challenged the notion of multigenerational curses. Yet in 1853 he anchored his rationale for a priesthood restriction in poor choices that Black people supposedly made as spirits in their premortal realm. It was a rationale perhaps designed to alleviate the theological pressure point that Young's explanation created. Pratt's description became a key alternative justification to divine curses, even though both reasonings continued to animate Latter-day Saint leaders' explanations for the restrictions for the next 130 years.[3]

For Pratt, the central question he hoped to address was the various conditions of human birth, with some born to wealth and privilege and others to poverty and deprivation. "Some are born among the people of God and are brought up in the right way; others are born among the heathen, and taught to worship idols," he explained. "Some spirits take bodies in the lineage of the chosen seed, through whom the priesthood is transferred, others receive bodies among the African negroes or in the lineage of Canaan whose descendants were cursed, pertaining to the priesthood," Pratt said, using book of Abraham shorthand to shore up his position.[4]

He then suggested that the Latter-day Saint teaching that all human beings were eternal and had existed as spirits before obtaining mortal bodies was an important understanding that helped to account for the various circumstances in which they entered mortality. Their choices in the pre-earth life, he believed, accounted for the conditions in which they were born on earth. "If rewards and punishments are the results of good and evil actions, then it would seem that the good and evil circumstances under which the spirits enter this world must depend upon the good and evil actions which they had done in the previous world."[5]

Despite his spirited rejection of slavery in 1852, his support of Black male voting rights, and his refusal to accept that Black people were cursed descendants of Cain, Pratt crafted his own explanation for a priesthood restriction, one that would endure among Latter-day Saints in various forms for more than a century. Pratt's version honored agency, a key component of the Latter-day Saint gospel plan, but imagined that Black people had exercised it in "evil" ways before coming to earth.[6]

Pratt's explanation was an expansion of an argument that fellow apostle Orson Hyde had made in 1845. Hyde did not mention priesthood but did suggest that decisions in the premortal realm accounted for the origins of the "African race." In Hyde's explanation "those spirits in heaven" that did not "take a very active part" in the war between Satan and Jesus were "required to come into the world and take bodies in the accursed lineage of Canaan; and hence the negro or African race."[7]

In 1869, Brigham Young denounced the idea of neutrality in the premortal realm as an explanation for black skin or the African race. He taught that "there was No Nutral spirits in Heaven at the time of the Rebelion. All took sides. . . . All spirits are pure that Come from the presence of God." He then reasserted his standard explanation for black skin: "The posterity of Cane are Black Because He commit Murder. He killed Abel & God set a Mark upon his posterity."[8]

In this regard, the debate between Orson Pratt and Brigham Young continued long after the legislative session ended. The two men gave life to the two competing explanations for the racial priesthood restrictions in the Church—explanations that continued to animate debates over the restrictions well into the twentieth century. Both explanations were grounded in an underlying assumption that Black people were inferior to white people and that white skin was normal and black skin was somehow cursed—a deterioration away from whiteness. Rather than trusting Jesus Christ when He told Joseph Smith,

ORSON PRATT AND A PREMORTAL EXPLANATION

"All flesh is mine, and I am no respecter of persons," these various explanations favored white flesh over other shades of flesh and implied that Jesus Christ was in fact a respecter of persons.

Despite Brigham Young's insistence to the contrary, the premortal explanation continued to be proffered by subsequent leaders. In 1885, Brigham H. Roberts, while serving as assistant mission president over the Southern States Mission, drew on the book of Abraham to posit that the descendants of Ham represented "that race . . . through which it is ordained those spirits that were not valiant in the great rebellion in heaven should come." He said that it was "through their indifference or lack of integrity to righteousness" that they "rendered themselves unworthy of the Priesthood and its powers, and hence it is withheld from them to this day."[9]

In 1907, as the premortal explanation gained ground among Latter-day Saints, Joseph Fielding Smith, then serving as assistant Church historian, argued that the teaching was "not the official position of the Church, merely the opinion of men."[10] Yet it persisted in various forms. In 1944, John A. Widtsoe attempted to navigate between the two competing explanations when he argued against neutrality and against Cain's murder of Abel as viable answers. "All who have been permitted to come upon this earth and take upon themselves bodies, accepted the plan of salvation," he said. Moreover, because Black people themselves "did not commit Cain's sin," a reason for the priesthood restriction had to involve something besides Cain's murder of Abel. "It is very probable," Widtsoe believed, "that in some way, unknown to us, the distinction harks back to the pre-existent state."[11]

Rather than question the racial restriction itself, leaders cast about for ways to justify it. Even though Joseph Fielding Smith had argued in 1907 that the premortal explanation was "merely the opinion of men," he resorted to it himself by the 1960s, although he altered it from "neutral" to "less valiant." In his *Answers to Gospel Questions*, he claimed that some premortal spirits "were not valiant" in the War in Heaven. As a result of "their lack of obedience," Black people came to earth "under restrictions," including a denial of the priesthood.[12]

In the 1840s, Joseph Smith had concluded that any differences between white and Black people was environmental: "Change their situation with the white & they would be like them," he argued.[13] He insisted in 1844 that "God hath created all men free and equal."[14] Yet, by the 1850s, both the curse of Cain and premortal explanations did not consider Black people to be theologically interchangeable with white people, nor did they give them equal status in life or in the eternities. Both explanations were grounded in an unfounded premise—that Black people were inferior and that black skin needed to be explained. White skin, in contrast, was perceived to be normal and in no need of explanation.

In 2013, in an essay approved by the First Presidency and Quorum of the Twelve Apostles, the Church renounced both explanations: "Today, the Church disavows the theories advanced in the past that black skin is a sign of divine disfavor or curse, or that it reflects unrighteous actions in a premortal life; that mixed-race marriages are a sin; or that blacks or people of any other race or ethnicity are inferior in any way to anyone else. Church leaders today unequivocally condemn all racism, past and present, in any form."[15]

CHAPTER 12

THE PRIESTHOOD AND TEMPLE RESTRICTIONS IN PRACTICE

"He died in full faith of the Gospel"

Even as Church leaders cast about for explanations, the implications for the racial restrictions were most directly felt among Black Latter-day Saints. They witnessed the space for full participation shrink across the course of their own lifetimes. Elijah and Mary Ann Adams Able migrated to Utah from Cincinnati, Ohio, in 1853, and both received rebaptism that same year as evidence of their rebirth in Christ in their new home. In 1857, the couple again committed themselves to their faith, this time joined by their oldest son, Moroni, with yet another baptism.[1]

In 1877, Mary Ann died, leaving Elijah alone. It is possible that Elijah and Mary Ann applied to Brigham Young to have their love for each other sealed for eternity, but if so that application escaped the written record other than a belated remembrance from Joseph F. Smith. Able had received his washing and anointing rituals in the Kirtland Temple and now hoped to receive the rest of his rituals in Salt Lake City. Even if Brigham Young had turned him down previously, the death of his wife Mary Ann likely compelled Able to try again.[2]

In 1879, he applied to John Taylor to receive his endowment and to be sealed to Mary Ann for eternity. Just a few months earlier he had been invited to speak at a gathering of the various quorums of the Seventies, with members from thirty-three quorums in attendance. As a member of the third quorum, Able "related some of the sayings of the prophet Joseph" in his talk, especially that Joseph Smith told him "that those who were called to the Melshizadec [*sic*] Priesthood and had magnified that calling would be sealed up unto eternal life."³

It may have been those very recollections that prompted Able to pursue his remaining temple rituals. It is not clear what Able understood about the racial restrictions at that point. He was not in Utah in 1852 when Brigham Young spoke to the legislature, and even if he had

Elijah Able, ordained to the priesthood in 1836

been, Young's speeches were never published. Leaders did begin to openly speak of the racial restrictions after that, but Able's oldest son Moroni had been ordained to the priesthood in 1871, so the restrictions played out unevenly in his family. His son Moroni received a deathbed ordination, a not uncommon practice in the nineteenth century. Such ordinations were administered as a final ritual designed to send the departing man into the spirit realm with priesthood authority as he continued his journey through the eternities.⁴

Moroni's health had been failing for some time, and a few days before he died, he "desired the administration of the Elders." While priesthood leaders gave Moroni a blessing for his sickness, they also "ordained [him] an Elder, for which he expressed his gratitude." There is no indication that Moroni's race was a factor in the decision.⁵

Perhaps in light of such experiences in his own family, Elijah Able appealed to John Taylor in 1879 to receive his remaining temple rituals. The ensuing investigation is an indication that the racial restrictions were not firmly in place as late as 1879. Even the leader of the Church, President John Taylor, was unsure how to proceed. If the restrictions were unambiguously in place, there would have been no need to scrutinize

THE PRIESTHOOD AND TEMPLE RESTRICTIONS

Able's request. Instead, John Taylor sent Apostle Joseph F. Smith to interview Able.[6]

In that interview, Able informed Joseph F. Smith that Joseph Smith had told him that "he was entitled to the priesthood and all the blessings." He recounted his ordination as an elder, his ministerial license from Joseph Smith, his washing and anointings in the Kirtland Temple, and his ordination as a Seventy.[7] Surviving sources in the Church History Library document the accuracy of Able's report.

Because of the overwhelming evidence in Able's favor, John Taylor decided to allow Able's priesthood to stand but denied him temple admission. He wondered if Able's priesthood was not like "many other things done in the early days of the Church," that were sometimes done without proper knowledge, but "as the Lord gave further light and revelation things were done with greater order." In John Taylor's mind the "greater order" was the racial restriction. He concluded that "what had been done through lack of knowledge, that was not altogether correct in detail, was allowed to remain."[8]

In John Taylor's assessment, Joseph Smith had erred in allowing Able the priesthood, and Brigham Young had revealed God's will when he declared Black people to be cursed descendants of Cain. With each new decision, the racial restrictions hardened in place, especially as each succeeding generation became reluctant to violate the precedent established under Brigham Young, even though Brigham Young's precedent violated the open priesthood and temple policies put in place under Joseph Smith.

Despite being denied the crowning rituals of his faith, Elijah Able remained faithful. In 1883, Joseph F. Smith set him apart to serve a third mission; he returned to Ohio to preach at the age of seventy-five.[9] His proselyting stint physically drained him, and he died within two weeks of his return. The *Deseret News* published his obituary, an atypical eulogy that recited his priesthood ordination dates. It noted that he passed away of "old age and debility, consequent upon exposure while laboring in the ministry in Ohio" and concluded that "he died in full faith of the Gospel."[10]

The obituary writer seemed to be speaking to the ages, challenging not only those of Able's day but also future Latter-day Saints to dare to refute Able's priesthood and his devotion to The Church of Jesus Christ of Latter-day Saints.

CHAPTER 13

A ONE-DROP POLICY

"Having tainted blood in her veins"

In 1836 in Claiborne County, Mississippi, a planter and enslaver named Lewis Foscue penned his last will and testament. He made special provisions for one of his enslaved girls, Rebecca Henrietta, who was also his daughter. Foscue wanted her set free following his death. Despite his best intentions, however, laws in Mississippi prevented enslavers from freeing their enslaved people without a special act of the state legislature.[1]

Rebecca Henrietta was likely only three or four years old when Foscue died and his wishes for her went unfulfilled. Her life thereafter took a variety of unexpected turns, not the least of which was gaining her freedom as an adult, joining The Church of Jesus Christ of Latter-day Saints, and being sealed to her husband in the Endowment House in Salt Lake City in 1863. Rebecca thus became one of only two known formerly enslaved people to be sealed to her spouse. It is a remarkable story that illustrates the uneven way that the developing racial restrictions played out in practice. Jane Manning James, in the meantime, appealed for her temple rituals but was repeatedly denied.

Following Lewis Foscue's death in 1836, an inventory of his estate valued Rebecca Henrietta at four hundred dollars. Rather than being freed, Rebecca was sold to a neighboring planter. She next appears in the historical record in 1860, this time living as a free woman in Cincinnati, Ohio. She somehow had gained her freedom and made her way to Cincinnati, a prominent hub on the Underground Railroad.[2]

It was in Cincinnati that Rebecca met Nathan Meads, a convert to the Church from Britain. It is likely that Nathan introduced Rebecca to the gospel, after which she embraced it with baptism in 1861.³ The newly married couple then made their way to Utah and settled in the Salt Lake Eleventh Ward, where they lived the rest of their lives. Even though the 1860 census listed Rebecca as "mulatto," an indication of her mixed racial heritage, all known public documents after that described her as white. In 1863, Rebecca received her endowment, after which she and Nathan had their love for each other sealed for eternity in the Endowment House. By all indications, they lived the rest of their lives as faithful Latter-day Saints.⁴

It is not clear what Rebecca's local leaders understood about her racial identity or when they came to know it, but in 1885, four years after her death, a member of her stake presidency described Nathan Meads as "white" and Rebecca as "quadroon," meaning that he believed she had at least one grandparent of African ancestry. He described the couple's children as "all very dark." He mentioned other people in the stake who were also of mixed ancestry and then indicated that he was "cognizant of all these having received their endowments here."⁵

Another person in the stake, Laura Berry, whose mother was white and whose father was described as "a very light mulatto," was aware of those other cases too and appealed for her temple rituals on similar grounds. Joseph E. Taylor, a counselor in Berry's stake presidency, sent the appeal to President John Taylor (no relation): "The question I desire to ask is, can you give this girl any privileges of a like character? The girl is very pretty and quite white and would not be suspected as having tainted blood in her veins unless her parentage was known."⁶

The letter represents the practical challenges that the racial restrictions created. In the nineteenth century, people understood race to somehow be passed in a person's blood. In the language of the day, they suggested that having African ancestry "tainted" a person's bloodline. The science of DNA has changed our understanding so that we now know how

A ONE-DROP POLICY

interrelated the human family actually is. As research geneticist Daniel J. Fairbanks explains, "As humans, everyone is related by common ancient ancestry" that traces to sub-Saharan Africa. DNA tells us that "ultimately, everyone is African."[7] Joseph Smith and Brigham Young were thus religiously *and* scientifically correct when they quoted Acts 17:26 to teach that God "hath made of one blood all nations of men for to dwell on all the face of the earth."

In attempting to enforce a racial restriction, however, the broad commonality of the human family got lost in the quest to shore up a mythical white purity measured in distance from blackness. That quest left leaders with impossible decisions to make as they attempted to determine how much African ancestry a person could have and still receive priesthood ordination and temple rituals. Should decisions be made based on appearance, as Joseph E. Taylor suggested, or something else? What shade of flesh qualified for inclusion, and what shade of flesh meant that a person should be excluded?

DNA teaches us that such questions were impossible to answer, given that a person who looks white may still have African ancestry and that the entire "human species originated in Africa" in the first place.[8] At the height of racial segregation in the United States, however, the nation became obsessed with what color of flesh deserved exclusion, and the Church followed along, inching toward a "one-drop" policy.

In 1896, following the U.S. Supreme Court's decision in *Plessy v. Ferguson*, which legalized separate but supposedly equal facilities, states had to decide exactly who should be segregated. What colors of flesh qualified for separate facilities such as drinking fountains, elevators, bus seats, swimming pools, theaters, train cars, and even cemeteries? Some states, such as Virginia, eventually adopted a "one-drop" policy, which meant that a person could have ninety-nine white ancestors and one Black ancestor (or "one drop" of African blood, as people described it at the time) and that person was legally defined as Black.[9]

Latter-day Saints grappled with similar questions. In 1900, George Q. Cannon, First Counselor in the First Presidency, led a "conversation between the First Presidency respecting the negro race." Cannon "asked President Snow if the question was not already decided," but President Snow "spoke as though it was not," an indication that even as late as 1900, the President of the Church, Lorenzo Snow, did not consider the racial restriction a settled matter. Cannon shared his perspective, a stance that moved the Church closer to adopting a "one-drop" policy of its own. Cannon believed "that however white a man may be and though every trace of negro blood be lost in his appearance, still if he were a descendant of that race in any degree he could not legally hold the priesthood."[10]

Surviving sources do not indicate if President Snow ever felt settled on the racial restrictions himself. He died just one year later, and it would fall to his successor, Joseph F. Smith, to decide. In 1907, under a reconstituted First Presidency, the Church adopted a "one-drop" policy of its own: "The descendants of Ham may receive baptism and confirmation," the First Presidency decided, "but no one known to have in his veins negro blood, (it matters not how remote a degree) can either have the Priesthood in any degree or the blessings of the Temple of God; no matter how otherwise worthy he may be."[11] Priesthood and temple denial was thus not based on worthiness, but the remotest degree of "negro blood" could thereafter disqualify a person. If "one drop" was the standard, however, DNA evidence makes it clear that there has never been a period of Latter-day Saint history without Black people admitted to the temple and ordained to the priesthood. It was a standard impossible to enforce.

The 1907 decision was designed to prevent having to continue to grapple with questions such as those Joseph E. Taylor posed concerning members of his stake with mixed racial ancestry. It also came in response to recurrent appeals from Jane Manning James, who with her husband and two boys was an 1847 pioneer into the Salt Lake Valley. She remained

A ONE-DROP POLICY

a committed Latter-day Saint but witnessed the space for full participation shrink across her own lifetime. She repeatedly petitioned Church leaders to receive the crowning rituals of her faith and was repeatedly denied.[12]

In 1884, she wrote to President John Taylor seeking temple admission. "I realize my race & color & cant expect my Endowments as others who are white," she wrote. "My race was handed down through the flood & God promised Abraham that in his seed all the nations of the earth should be blest & as this is the fullness of all dispensations is there no blessing for me?"[13]

It was a haunting question, grounded in universalistic ideals from the early decades of the Church and drawn from sacred texts. Rather than the problematic reading of the book of Abraham verses regarding Egyptus that leaders drew on to justify racial exclusion, James instead focused on the Lord's promise to Abraham that his seed would "bear this ministry and Priesthood unto all nations," and that in his seed "shall all the families of the earth be blessed" (Abraham 2:9, 11). James took such sentiments at face value and wondered, "Is there no blessing for me?" No reply from John Taylor is known to exist, but James maintained her appeals.[14]

Leaders did allow James and other Black Latter-day Saints to perform baptisms for their deceased ancestors and friends in the Endowment House and granted James a limited-use recommend to attend the Logan and Salt Lake temples after that. Even still, James wanted all of her temple blessings. She insisted that in Nauvoo, Emma Smith had invited her to be sealed into Joseph and Emma's family line in an adoption ceremony. In response, in 1894, Church leaders attempted to appease her, this time with an unprecedented ceremony wherein she was "attached" by proxy to Joseph Smith Jr. as a servant. It was a ceremony that reinforced racial inferiority, and so James continued to request full and equal temple privileges.[15]

James's ongoing rejections notwithstanding, she and her brother Isaac Lewis Manning, who had joined her in Salt

Lake City by 1892, shared a place of respect among Latter-day Saints. They had both worked for Joseph Smith in the Nauvoo Mansion House and were highly regarded because of that connection alone. James and Manning were given prominent and reserved seats in the Salt Lake Tabernacle "near the front in the center of the building," where the *Deseret News* reported that "Jane made cushions for the seats, and the old couple and their friends had the exclusive right to the seats."[16]

One article even noted that they were "conspicuous figures at all of the annual and semiannual conferences of the church and occupied the only cushioned seats in the vast auditorium, aside from those occupied by the leading officials of the organization."[17] Another story honored their faithful attendance at the semiannual gatherings and observed that Manning and James had not "missed a conference meeting and but few Sunday services'" over the course of their years in the Church.[18]

When James died in 1908, President Joseph F. Smith spoke at her funeral, and when Manning passed away in 1911, Joseph F. Smith spoke at his funeral too. It was a symbol of the regard with which both pioneer Latter-day Saints were held. They were given prominent seats in the Tabernacle but barred from the temple.[19]

CHAPTER 14

THE RESTRICTIONS HARDEN IN PLACE

"Not to make any special effort to convert them"

Just a few months after Jane Manning James's death in 1908, President Joseph F. Smith and other leaders again gathered to discuss matters of race. This time a letter from the recently returned mission president in South Africa, Ralph A. Badger, prompted the meeting. "What shall be done where people tainted with negro blood embrace the Gospel?" Badger questioned. His missionaries had recently baptized the son of a Zulu chief who wanted to take the gospel to the rest of his group. Badger further wondered if the gospel should be preached at all "to the native tribes" of South Africa.[1]

In response to Badger's inquiry, Joseph F. Smith recited for the gathered council the stories of Elijah Able and Jane Manning James—specifically their appeals for temple blessings. Joseph F. Smith recounted Able's story as precedent, but he remembered it differently than when he had personally interviewed Able in 1879 and then later set him apart as a missionary in 1883. In 1895, Joseph F. Smith had reminded leaders that Able had been ordained "at Kirtland under the direction of the Prophet Joseph Smith," but in 1904 he claimed that Able's priesthood was a mistake that "was never corrected."[2] Now in 1908, he solidified the racial restrictions in place when he claimed that Able's "ordination was declared null and void by the Prophet himself."[3]

In 1908, Joseph F. Smith thus created a new memory for the Church moving forward. This new memory erased from collective Latter-day Saint history the Black pioneers who complicated the racial story. In the new memory, priesthood and temples had always been white, and the racial restrictions had been in place from the beginning.

As for preaching among Black people, the council decided that missionaries "should not take the initiative in proselyting among the negro people, but if negroes or people tainted with negro blood apply for baptism themselves they might be admitted to Church membership in the understanding that nothing further can be done for them."[4]

That same year, a missionary then working in South Africa indicated a similar approach on that continent: "Although many of Africa's people are colored," he wrote, "we work only among Europeans, and have made great headway," he said. Then, without a hint of irony, he added that missionaries in South Africa had to "battle against" misperceptions that people there held against the Church. He stated that "a large part of our work is to remove prejudice, which is very strong."[5]

Even the Northern States Mission moved in the same direction. In 1909, the mission president there reported that three Black Latter-day Saint families lived within mission boundaries: one in Oshkosh, Wisconsin, another in Minneapolis, Minnesota, and a third in Great Bend, Indiana. Even though they were deemed to be "good faithful people," when white investigators attended, the Black families were "so much in evidence in our meetings" that the investigators lost interest in a church that permitted integrated worship. In response, the mission president instructed his missionaries to stop preaching "among the colored people" and had done so for the past seven years.[6]

By the turn of the twentieth century, Church leaders deliberately curtailed mission outreach among people of Black African ancestry despite the scriptural injunctions to preach "unto every creature." Such thinking became so entrenched among leaders and members alike that it was used on occasion to justify segregated Sunday worship in some locations and shunning of Black Latter-day Saints in others.

William and Marie Graves, two Black converts in

THE RESTRICTIONS HARDEN IN PLACE

Oakland, California, for example, visited Atlanta, Georgia, in 1920, where Marie hoped to introduce her friends to her chosen faith. When she showed up on Sunday to the Atlanta chapel, a branch leader invited Marie and her friends outside and let them know that the church had been "dedicated by the white people of the south." He made it clear that Marie and her friends were not welcome to stay. "I never had nothing to hurt me like that in all of my life," Marie wrote to President Heber J. Grant, recounting the profound rejection she felt. It was rejection accompanied by embarrassment at having invited her friends to attend her church and then not being allowed to stay.[7] Marie and her husband, nonetheless, returned to Oakland and continued to worship in integrated services there for the rest of their lives.[8]

Rather than inform the leaders in Atlanta that they were in the wrong, however, President Grant asked the California mission president to let Marie know that "in the south we must bear in mind the color line is drawn between the white and colored races" and that if "Oakland suddenly become populated thickly by negroes, evidently the same color line would have to be drawn there" as well. "We should bear in mind," he told the California mission president, "that our mission is not directly to the negro race."[9]

There are thus reasons why the Church became known as a white church in the twentieth century. In Missouri in the 1830s, Latter-day Saints had been accused of opening "an asylum for rogues and vagabonds and free blacks" and of even promoting black "ascendancy over the whites." Similar accusations continued for the rest of the century. During the same time span, Church leaders moved incrementally away from their own Black members toward whiteness and its corresponding acceptability. It was a racial passage, however, that came with a price. That price included racial prejudice, policies, teachings, and practices that became tightly woven into the fabric of the Church and would take another seventy years to begin to unravel.

CHAPTER 15

A LACK OF CONSENSUS FOR CHANGE

"I think the Lord segregated the Negro"

As the twentieth century wore on, leaders became increasingly convinced that the Church's racial restrictions had been in place from the beginning and that they stretched back through the foggy mists of time to the eternities. Yet, even as the racial practices, policies, and teachings became fixed in place, some Church leaders questioned their origins and advocated for reform, while other leaders reinforced the restrictions. This lack of consensus ensured that the restrictions would endure for most of the twentieth century.

In 1949, the First Presidency referred to the Church's racial teachings as "doctrine" for the first time and suggested that the restrictions had "always" been in place, a signal as to how entrenched the racial teachings had become. "The attitude of the Church with reference to Negroes remains as it has always stood. It is not a matter of the declaration of a policy but of direct commandment from the Lord," the Church leaders declared. The "doctrine of the Church" on priesthood and race was in place "from the days of its organization," they professed.[1] The First Presidency said nothing of the original Black priesthood holders, an indication of how thoroughly reconstructed memory had come to replace verifiable facts.

Just five years later, the United States Supreme Court handed down a landmark decision in *Brown v. Board of Education*, one in which it overturned segregation as valid. In the wake of that decision, Elder Mark E. Petersen of the Quorum of the Twelve Apostles gave a talk at Brigham Young University in which he upheld segregation as not only valid but of divine origins. "I think the Lord segregated the Negro,"

Petersen said, "and who is man to change that segregation?"[2] As the United States moved slowly toward civil rights, some Latter-day Saint leaders ensconced themselves behind racial barriers.

Adding to the doctrinal air of the restrictions, four years later, Elder Bruce R. McConkie, then a member of the First Council of the Seventy, published a popular and authoritatively titled book, *Mormon Doctrine*. In it he included entries on Cain, Ham, Negroes, and what he called a divinely ordered "Caste System." His explanations on those subjects helped to codify racial teachings as well as extend the corresponding restrictions forward.

"As a result of his rebellion, Cain was cursed with a dark skin," McConkie wrote; "he became the father of the Negroes, and those spirits who are not worthy to receive the priesthood are born through his lineage."[3] His explanations offered nothing new but were significant nonetheless because he collected the old teachings together, organized them into an encyclopedic volume that became wildly popular among Latter-day Saints, elevated them to an official status under the title of *Doctrine,* and ensured their republication into the twenty-first century.

McConkie's positions, like Petersen's before him, also marked a conservative retrenchment in response to societal changes taking place in the United States. By the time he published *Mormon Doctrine*, the Montgomery Bus Boycott had already desegregated public transportation in Montgomery, Alabama, and U.S. President Dwight D. Eisenhower had called out the National Guard in order to integrate Little Rock Central High School in Arkansas. In contrast, McConkie's entry on what he described as a divinely designed "Caste System" attempted to shore up segregation.

For McConkie, caste represented a system in which racial "restrictions and *segregation* are right and proper and have the approval of the Lord." In his estimation, "the whole negro race have been cursed with a black skin, the mark of

Cain, so they can be identified as a caste apart, a people with whom the other descendants of Adam should not intermarry."[4] McConkie further explained that "negroes are not equal with other races where the receipt of certain spiritual blessings are concerned, particularly the priesthood and temple blessings."[5]

Church President David O. McKay was uncomfortable with McConkie's book and its authoritative title and so he commissioned a committee to investigate. Two senior Apostles, Mark E. Petersen and Marion G. Romney, documented what they considered to be 1,067 errors and recommended it not be republished.[6] It did temporarily go out of print, but after making revisions, none of which changed the entries on Cain, Caste System, Ham, or Negroes, McConkie republished it. In 1979, he added information on the priesthood revelation under the heading for "Negroes" and modified his entry for Cain but still asserted that "Cain, Ham, and the whole negro race have been cursed with a black skin." *Mormon Doctrine* continued to be available for purchase with such claims intact up through 2010, when Deseret Book removed it from print.[7]

As civil rights demonstrations in the United States increased in the 1960s, the Church again struck a conservative tone. In 1969, it issued another First Presidency statement that linked the priesthood and temple bans to "Joseph Smith and all succeeding presidents of the Church." The reasons this time were "known to God" but were "not made fully known to man." The then President of the Church, David O. McKay, said that the "seeming discrimination by the Church toward the Negro is not something which originated with man; but goes back into the beginning with God." Gone as explanations were the curse of Cain and subpar valiancy in the premortal existence. In their place was a new "we don't know" explanation, which in the late twentieth and early twenty-first century came to replace the earlier rationales.[8]

Even as such statements publicly reinforced the restrictions, a lack of consensus among senior leaders prevailed. As early as 1954, President David O. McKay stipulated in a private interview with Sterling M. McMurrin, a philosophy professor at the University of Utah, that "there is no doctrine in this church and there never was a doctrine in the church to the effect that the Negroes are under any kind of a divine curse." Instead, McKay said it was "a practice, not a doctrine and the practice will some day be changed. And that's all there is to it."[9]

Hugh B. Brown, a counselor to President McKay in the First Presidency, agreed. In his estimation, if it was a practice not a doctrine, then leaders should remove it by policy vote. He reasoned that because there was no revelation that began the racial bans, no revelation was needed to end them. He worked behind the scenes throughout the 1960s to overturn the restrictions but was blocked by other leaders who suggested a revelation was necessary to undo what some considered to be long ingrained teachings, which they traced in their minds to the eternities.[10] Harold B. Lee, for example, insisted that the restrictions were fixed in place and worked to ensure Black people were not admitted to BYU in the fear that it would result in interracial dating and marriage.[11]

There were similar disagreements over the civil rights movement then dominating politics in the United States. Hugh B. Brown spoke in favor of civil rights at general conference in 1963 and reinforced ideals of "full civil equality for all of God's children." He declared that in the Church there was "no doctrine, belief, or practice, that is intended to deny the enjoyment of full civil rights by any person regardless of race, color, or creed."[12] In contrast, four years later, also in general conference, Elder Ezra Taft Benson suggested that "the so-called civil rights movement as it exists today is used as a Communist program for revolution in America."[13]

With such opposing views animating the perspectives of various leaders, the racial restrictions remained in force. As early as 1963, however, Elder Spencer W. Kimball signaled an open attitude for change: "The doctrine or policy has not varied in my memory," Kimball acknowledged. "I know it could. I know the Lord could change his policy and release the ban and forgive the possible error which brought about the deprivation."[14] It is no coincidence, then, that the forgiveness of which Kimball spoke ultimately came with him at the helm.

CHAPTER 16

RACIAL RESTRICTIONS AND THE INTERNATIONAL CHURCH

"I am satisfied that the Lord wants this brother to receive the priesthood"

In 1947, Heber C. Meeks, president of the Southern States Mission, penned a letter to the First Presidency of the Church: George Albert Smith, J. Reuben Clark, and David O. McKay. Meeks's letter encapsulated well the challenges the Church's racial policies presented in the twentieth century, not just in the United States but especially in international locations where generations of mixed racial marriages made it impossible to disentangle African ancestry from most people's family trees. Meeks had just returned from an exploratory trip to Cuba, where the Church hoped to send future missionaries.[1]

Meeks wondered, given the Church's racial policies, if it would be possible "to find, with any degree of certainty, groups of pure white people."[2] In his report to the First Presidency, he highlighted what he perceived to be the key problem: "the negro situation in Cuba." Meeks explained that Cubans had "intermarried freely" and noted that accurate records did not exist "to determine who has negro blood among the average Cuban."[3]

What Meeks said for Cuba was true for most of Latin America. In fact, far more enslaved people from Africa arrived in Latin America than in the U.S. and Canada; over several generations they mixed with people of European and Indigenous descent without the same concern over segregation that prevailed in the United States. Brazil is a notable example. In 1947, the First Presidency acknowledged that "the races are badly mixed in Brazil, and no color line is drawn among the mass of the people. The result is . . . that a great part of the population of Brazil is colored."[4]

As the Church opened or expanded missionary efforts in these countries, it attempted various strategies designed to limit gospel outreach to people of African ancestry. In Brazil, it initially concentrated on people of European descent and developed approaches to try to limit contact with those who were suspected of having African ancestry. Missionaries might ask to see family photos of those who expressed interest in their message or engage with them about their family history, and if evidence surfaced of potential African ancestry, they simply moved on to find new people to teach.[5]

One mission president, Rulon S. Howells, even developed a "lineage lesson" used in Brazil to attempt to determine ethnicity and prevent priesthood ordination of those of African descent. The extra lesson asked missionaries to question potential converts if they knew "if any of your ancestors were Negro or descendants of Negroes," and if they answered "no," to then request that the investigator tell their local leaders if they were to "discover that one of your ancestors was Negro" at some future time.[6]

Despite such efforts, people of African ancestry were inevitably baptized, and some of them were ordained to the priesthood. Men in Mexico, Ecuador, Honduras, Columbia, and Brazil all experienced the restrictions in different ways as missionaries and local leaders attempted to navigate racial boundaries designed to exclude rather than include. As in the United States, they learned the impossibilities of assessing racial ancestry according to the way a person looked or based on skin color.[7]

In 1958 in Mexico, Benigno Cobos and his wife María de la Cruz embraced the gospel in Veracruz, where American missionaries presided over the small branch. Missionaries refused to ordain Cobos to the priesthood, however, because in their eyes his dark skin was evidence of African ancestry. They even forbade him to pray at church and publicly reprimanded him for trying to help clean the sacrament trays one day. Despite such racism, Cobos persisted.[8]

After he and his family moved to Mexico City, the local Mexican leadership ordained him an elder in 1973. They were unfazed by Cobos's dark skin and welcomed him into church service. Cobos and his family then traveled to the Mesa Arizona Temple and were sealed together as a family in 1977. Cobos's skin color did not change over time; the difference was in the racial perceptions of those in authority over him. The American missionaries believed he was Black, while fellow members in Mexico City saw him as brown like themselves.[9]

In Honduras similar stories played out, sometimes with American missionaries offending baptized members with the racial designations that they assigned based on their own understandings. One missionary who taught Roberto Ocampo the gospel in Honduras, for example, described him as having "a very dark skin color and his hair was black and kinky in appearance." Because of ongoing questions over Ocampo's ethnicity, missionaries asked their mission president, Milton E. Smith, to conduct the baptismal interview. Smith found no reason to bar Ocampo from baptism, and the missionaries baptized him in January 1970.[10]

They failed, however, to tell Ocampo about the racial priesthood restriction. As a newly baptized member, he learned of the restriction through observation. "I noticed that all the others who had been baptized were receiving the priesthood," Ocampo later recalled, "and I was not being ordained." When he inquired into the matter, the missionaries explained to Ocampo their reservations about his potential African ancestry. Ocampo immediately saw the policy for what it was: "I said it was unjust that everyone else had the priesthood, and we could not have it."[11]

He eventually talked to his grandmother about his family history and she assured him, "You do not have black blood." That assurance was enough to satisfy the mission president, who personally ordained Ocampo an elder in February 1971.

Later, while serving as bishop, however, Ocampo came to question his grandmother's claim and wrote to Salt Lake City with his reservations. As one member of the Seventy was preparing to travel to Honduras and potentially release Ocampo as bishop, the First Presidency announced the 1978 revelation, making the trip pointless.[12]

In Ecuador, a similar situation developed in the case of Guillermo Cuesta, a 1966 convert. In Cuesta's case, the missionaries did discuss the priesthood restriction with him, but he simply explained that he was of Lebanese descent. That satisfied the missionaries for the time being, and they recommended him for ordination. In the meantime, they met another family who they began to teach but who quickly rejected their message once they learned of the racial restrictions. This family was proud of their African heritage and found the Church's policies offensive. To the missionaries' dismay, they also learned that Cuesta was immediately related to this particular family, which indicated that Cuesta was also of African descent.[13]

Not sure how to proceed, the missionaries asked Elder Spencer W. Kimball, who was then visiting Ecuador, to meet Cuesta and discuss the matter with him. Elder Kimball agreed, and on the appointed day emerged from a seemingly endless interview with Cuesta to tell the missionaries, "I am satisfied that the Lord wants this brother to receive the priesthood." That same day, Elder Kimball performed the ordination. The missionaries struggled to make sense of the situation: Elder Kimball had ordained a seemingly Black man to the priesthood in 1966, but the fact that an Apostle performed the ordination meant that no one questioned its validity thereafter.[14]

In Brazil, Eduardo Contieri's situation was different. He understood himself to be of European descent and looked white. He was baptized in 1963 and soon became branch president. In his new calling he urged branch members to engage in family history research and decided to lead by example. To his own surprise, however, he found evidence of African ancestry in his family tree. Dismayed, he let Church leaders in Brazil know of his discovery, and he was shortly thereafter released as branch president and his priesthood was suspended. The situation was upsetting not only to Contieri and his family but to branch members as well. Should the ordinances he performed as branch president be invalidated? It raised a variety of thorny questions.[15]

For the time being, Contieri was told not to exercise his priesthood in public, but within the walls of his own home it was allowed. He thus continued to bless his family. By 1971, the case came before the First Presidency, who decided to remove even the public suspension of Contieri's priesthood, a decision that then served as an important precedent. In the wake of the Contieri case, men in Brazil who discovered African ancestry *after* they had received the priesthood were allowed to remain priesthood holders. In fact, in 1973, Elder Howard W. Hunter traveled to Brazil and ordained Contieri a bishop over the São Paulo I Ward, five years before the 1978 revelation.[16]

In Colombia, a similar situation occurred, but this time with someone of apparent African descent. It was just a few months before the June 1978 revelation. The branch president over the Bucaramanga, Colombia, branch ordained Horacio Insignares, a person of African descent, to the priesthood. The branch president based his decision on devotion, not race, especially as he considered Insignares to be one of the most faithful men in the branch. American missionaries, disturbed by such a decision, alerted the mission president and called for the branch president's excommunication. The mission president, Kirt Olson, was uncertain what to do. As he recalled, "I knew the branch president was a good man, and I certainly had respect and appreciation for the black member who was given the priesthood." He also worried about potentially provoking a rift in the branch depending on how he handled the situation.[17]

Olson called Church President Spencer W. Kimball, who kindly indicated that Insignares was a "good man" who "has the priesthood. Just tell him that he can't use his priesthood right now." Following these instructions, Olson advised Insignares not to use his priesthood for the time being. Just a few months later, following the 1978 revelation, Olson once again called President Kimball for advice. Should he reordain Insignares to the priesthood? He wondered what now needed to be done in his case. "Just phone that man and tell him that he can now start using his priesthood," President Kimball advised. "He already has the priesthood so no additional ordination is needed." In 1981, just three years later, when the Bucaramanga District became a stake in Colombia, Insignares became the stake president, one of the first stake presidents of African descent in the world.[18]

As these examples indicate, the racial restrictions provided challenges in Latin America that local and general leaders attempted to navigate in ways that deferred to people's own understanding of their racial heritage. Leaders also started to make decisions based more on a person's devotion to God rather than attempt to enforce a "one-drop" policy or decide what shade of skin should be included or excluded.

Meanwhile in Africa, men and women there organized entire congregations based on encounters some of them had had with the Book of Mormon, Church literature, or members of the Church. Joseph Johnson is one such example. In the 1960s, he read a variety of Church publications and experienced heavenly manifestations that drew him to develop a congregation in Ghana along with fellow believers. They then waited on leaders from Salt Lake to recognize their efforts. As Johnson recalled, "We met no matter what the weather. We were singing the songs of Zion, using the LDS books and striving to obey all commandments of our Heavenly Father and also learning to emulate the shining examples of the church in America, especially the early pioneers of the Church."[19]

Similar congregations formed in Nigeria. The Holy Spirit

converted over fifteen thousand people in Africa without missionaries or administrative oversight from Salt Lake City.[20] The Lord's Spirit reached out to religious seekers, regardless of skin color, and made it evident that the spirit of conversion was no respecter of persons. It was yet another way that the Church's racial barriers were standing in the way of the Savior's mandate to preach the gospel unto "every creature."

Especially after the Church announced a temple in São Paulo, Brazil, in 1975, the gravity of the matter became abundantly clear. Church leaders flew to Brazil and met faithful Black Latter-day Saints who donated their hard-earned money toward an edifice they knew they would not be allowed to enter. It tugged at the heartstrings of leaders and helped them to refashion their perspective. Their questions transitioned from "How will we keep people of mixed racial ancestry out of the temple?" to "How can we let them in?"[21]

In fact, Elder LeGrand Richards pointed to the São Paulo temple as a key factor moving the Church forward. "Down in Brazil, there is so much Negro blood in the population," he explained just after the June 1978 revelation, "that it's hard to get leaders that don't have Negro blood in them. We just built a temple down there. It's going to be dedicated in October. All those people with Negro blood in them have been raising the money to build that temple. If we don't change, then they can't even use it." As Elder Richards put it, the situation weighed on President Kimball, who "worried about it, and prayed a lot about it." It was a significant factor leading to the revelation.[22]

By the time that President Kimball dedicated the São Paulo Brazil Temple in October 1978, Black Saints were present—*inside* the temple.

PHASE THREE

A RETURN TO RACIAL INCLUSIVITY

CHAPTER 17

THE 1978 REVELATION

"The Happiest Day of My Life"

Freda Lucretia Magee was nine years old when Ernest Koepsel, a Latter-day Saint missionary, baptized her in a creek outside Tylertown, Mississippi, on June 28, 1909. Her sister Vander and brothers Percy and Flanders were baptized on the same day. Her parents Samuel and Ardella Magee had previously converted, and now their oldest children were joining too.[1]

Freda thus grew up in a Latter-day Saint home, filled with scripture study and prayer. Even still, it would be sixty-nine years and twenty-three days from the date of her baptism before Freda was allowed to enter a Latter-day Saint temple. When she finally did, it was on July 21, 1978, exactly one month and thirteen days after the public announcement of what came to be called "the priesthood revelation" in Latter-day Saint circles. Freda had traveled roughly one thousand miles from New Orleans, Louisiana, to the Washington D.C. Temple to be sealed by proxy to her husband Pierre Rudolph Beaulieu, who had died six years earlier. She remembered it as "the happiest day" of her life.[2]

Events of June 1 of that year, far away in Salt Lake City, made Freda's happiest day possible. "Revelations will probably never come unless they are desired," President Spencer W. Kimball had written to his son Edward Kimball in 1963. "I believe most revelations would come when a man is on his top toes, reaching as high as he can for something which he knows he needs, and then there bursts upon him the answer to his problems."[3] It was a discerning description of the process he would follow ten years later when he became prophet.

President Kimball reached for a revelation almost as soon as he became prophet in 1973. For him, that included doing the work of studying the issue out in his own mind, learning the history of the restrictions for himself, understanding the various justifications that had been offered over the years, and digging into the issue in depth. It included overcoming his own preconceived opinions and understandings as well as working behind the scenes to create consensus among Church leaders. "I had a great deal to fight," he later recalled, "myself, largely, because I had grown up with this thought that Negroes should not have the priesthood and I was prepared to go all the rest of my life until my death and fight for it and defend it as it was."[4]

For President Kimball, a part of his "fight" was dismantling the constructs of racism he had been taught from his youth. Historical precedent and statements from past leaders were stacked against change. As his son Edward Kimball explained, "In a sense, the past prophets of the Church stood arrayed against this decision. The wisdom of the dead often seems loftier than the word of an imperfect living spokesman."[5]

Indeed, President Kimball's counselor in the First Presidency, Marion G. Romney, who knew President Kimball was wrestling with the matter, later stated, "I did not expect him to get an answer. If the decision had been left to me, I would have felt that we've always had that policy and we would stick to it no matter what the opposition."[6] Sheer inertia and the weight of what many considered settled doctrine in 1978 worked to President Kimball's disadvantage. Yet, as his son put it, "It was not enough just to wait until the Lord saw fit to take the initiative: the scripture admonished him to ask and to knock if he wanted to know for himself."[7]

President Kimball opened his mind to new possibilities and sought new sources of information, including that from leading scholars on the question.[8] Historians began to chip away at the accepted story, that the racial restrictions were in place from the beginning and were of divine origins known only to God. Most significantly, in 1973, Lester E. Bush published a seminal article in *Dialogue: A Journal of Mormon Thought*,

THE 1978 REVELATION

which was influential in changing existing assumptions. He found no evidence of Joseph Smith's involvement in the racial restrictions but situated their beginnings in Utah Territory with Brigham Young. His evidence opened new possibilities.[9]

President Kimball searched the scriptures as well. According to his son Edward, he concluded that the restrictions "did not come from explicit scriptures but rather from interpretations by various Church leaders." It was a conclusion that matched an earlier study conducted under President David O. McKay that found that the "priesthood ban had no clear basis in scripture."[10]

With the historical and scriptural assumptions regarding the restrictions on unstable ground, President Kimball began to build consensus among senior leaders. He was aware of the way that the issue had been divisive during President McKay's administration, and he wanted to avoid a similar outcome. In March 1978, President Kimball told his counselors that he felt impressed to lift the racial restrictions. His counselors expressed support, but President Kimball "felt unity within the leadership was important," and so he drew the Quorum of the Twelve Apostles in as well. He met with leaders individually as well as discussing the matter collectively. He "urged a concerted effort from all of them to learn the will of the Lord. He suggested they engage in concerted individual fasting and prayer."[11]

President Kimball spent considerable time in the temple seeking inspiration himself. As he recalled, "I remember very vividly the day after day that I walked over to the temple and ascended up to the fourth floor where we have our solemn assemblies, where we have our meetings of the Twelve and the Presidency. And after everybody had gone out of the temple, I knelt and prayed. And I prayed with such fervency, I tell you! I knew that something was before us that was extremely important to many of the children of God."[12]

On June 1, the First Presidency and Quorum of the Twelve Apostles met in the Salt Lake Temple and President Kimball led them in prayer. He sought the Lord's confirmation for his plan to return priesthood ordination to all men regardless of race or ethnicity. As Elder Bruce R. McConkie recalled, as President Kimball prayed "some of the Brethren were weeping. All were sober and somewhat overcome. When President Kimball stood up, several of the Brethren, in turn, threw their arms around him."[13]

Elder L. Tom Perry described the experience this way: "While he was praying we had a marvelous experience. We had just a unity of feeling. The nearest I can describe it is that it was much like what has been recounted as happening at the dedication of the Kirtland Temple. I felt something like the rushing of wind." Elder David B. Haight recalled, "The Spirit touched each of our hearts with the same message in the same way. Each was witness to a transcendent heavenly event." Elder Gordon B. Hinckley felt similarly. He was overcome with a "strong conviction that this change was a revelation from God."[14]

In October 1978, President N. Eldon Tanner of the First Presidency presented the revelation to the worldwide Church for sustaining vote. It was the only time that any teaching or policy regarding the racial restrictions was presented to the Church for inclusion in the scriptural canon, the formal process by which revelations become scripture in the Latter-day Saint tradition. It is the official means by which the leaders and the people of faith become united in revelation.

The revelation restored people of African descent to the priesthood and returned the Church to its universal roots. It brought Church policy and practice back into compliance with the scriptures of the Restoration and reestablished what had been lost from the early decades of the Church when Black men were ordained to the priesthood and the First Presidency had anticipated welcoming people "of every color" into the temple at Nauvoo.[15] It confirmed that Church doctrine was indeed grounded in inclusivity.

For Freda Lucretia Magee Beaulieu, the 1978 revelation made possible the happiest day of her life. Her experience is an important reminder that the so called "priesthood ban" also restricted women and men of African descent from the temple, not merely Black men from the priesthood. It prevented Black men and women from missionary service as well, even though Elijah Able, the faith's first Black priesthood holder, served three missions for the Church.

Freda was likely unaware of such policies when she was baptized in 1909, but as an adult she came to understand that her race barred her from temple admission no matter her devotion to God. There was no commandment that she could live any more devoutly than she already did in order to change that. Before 1978, Freda could answer the temple recommend questions exactly the same as a white person, and the white person would be admitted and Freda denied.[16]

After her baptism, Freda recalled growing up in a gospel-centered home. It was the place where she learned to read the scriptures, pray, observe the Word of Wisdom, and pay her tithing. "We always had prayer morning and night and scripture study before going to bed," she recalled. "Once in a while missionaries would come by and spend some time teaching us more about the gospel," she remembered.[17]

Freda also recalled her father's faithfulness in always sending his tithing into the local branch. As she described it, "My parents taught us the principle of tithing. When my father was teaching school our tithing was sent in regularly." After he retired from schoolteaching, Samuel turned to farming, and as Freda recounted, "when the crops were gathered and sold, the tithing was sent in."[18]

When Freda was twenty-five years old, she married Robert H. May Jr., who had children of his own. He was not kind to Freda and forbid her to go to church because, Freda explained, "he hated Mormons." Even still she clung to the principles she had learned as a child. As she described it, "I continued my scripture study and prayers. When I was able to get a little money, I put a portion away in my trunk, for tithing." When her husband's children were old enough to care for themselves, Freda divorced Robert May and moved back to her childhood home. "The money I had been saving in my trunk all those years was joyfully turned in to the church," she recalled.[19]

Freda Beaulieu

Freda eventually moved to New Orleans, where she met and married the love of her life, Rudolph Beaulieu. "This was a very happy marriage," she said. "Rudolph was Catholic but he allowed me to attend my church. In fact, he encouraged me to go when possible. He encouraged me to pay my tithing. Rudolph was a kind man and so good to me," she said.[20]

When Freda fell ill in 1944, it was Rudolph who tracked down Latter-day Saint leaders in New Orleans and invited them into the couple's home to give his wife a blessing. Freda had not realized that there was a branch of the Church that met in New Orleans. She subscribed to the missionary magazine, the *Liahona*, and sent her tithing into the mission office in Atlanta, but had been unaware of the local branch. Somehow Rudolph found the branch leaders in New Orleans and called to request a blessing for Freda.[21]

President Robert B. Evans of the New Orleans Branch, accompanied by Parker P. Warner, first counselor in the South Louisiana District presidency, arrived at the Beaulieu home somewhat unsure that they were in the correct place because they knew of no Black Saints in New Orleans. Warner described the scene this way:

> Sister Freda Beaulieu carried on her face an expression of mixed feelings—anxiety was giving way to confidence which was to be succeeded by relief and gratefulness. President Evans talked to her for a few minutes and she told us she had been a Latter-day Saint all her life, her

THE 1978 REVELATION

parents having joined the Church in Mississippi before her time. She had been in New Orleans for many years but did not know of the branch, and having fallen ill, she had written to the mission headquarters in Atlanta in an effort to locate the elders.[22]

While Freda waited for a reply from Atlanta she remained in bed and sometimes "suffered intense pain." Warner and Evans then gave her a blessing, an experience that made a significant impression on both men.[23] "Never in all my life had I felt such confidence in the healing power of faith as I did in that home," Warner declared. "The faith which led Sister Beaulieu to write to Atlanta and wait patiently through her suffering until those bearing the priesthood could reach her and give her a blessing, was such as I had not witnessed in all my experience. I was astonished at my own confidence in the blessing I pronounced on her head, and when we had sealed that blessing in the name of the Lord, I said to her with all the assurance of one who has absolute knowledge, 'Sister Freda, I know you will soon be well.' She replied, 'Yes, I know it, too; thank you.'"[24] Warner checked back on Freda a few days later: "'I have been feeling fine,' she said. 'The next day after you were here I got out of bed and have been well ever since.'"[25]

In 1982, leaders of the New Orleans Stake asked Freda to speak at stake conference. She wrote her talk out but was too nervous to deliver it, so she stood in front of the large congregation as someone read it in her behalf. It was in that talk that she declared July 21, 1978, to be the happiest day of her life. It was the day that Robert B. Evans, the branch president who had found her sick in bed in 1944, stood in as proxy for her beloved Rudolph as the couple was sealed together for eternity in the Washington D.C. Temple.[26]

CHAPTER 18

POST-REVELATION JUSTIFICATIONS

"We spoke with a limited understanding"

Within months of the June 1978 revelation, Elder Bruce R. McConkie spoke at Brigham Young University. "It doesn't make a particle of difference what anybody ever said about the Negro matter before the first day of June of this year," he announced. "Forget everything that I have said, or what President Brigham Young or George Q. Cannon, or whomsoever has said in days past that is contrary to the present revelation. We spoke with a limited understanding and without the light and knowledge that now has come into the world."[1] It was a statement that suggested that prior teachings on race lacked the "light and knowledge" that revelation represents to Latter-day Saints.

How could this happen in The Church of Jesus Christ of Latter-day Saints? How could teachings "without the light and knowledge" that the 1978 revelation represented come to so firmly replace founding precepts of the Restoration centered on God's universal love? How could racial priesthood and temple restrictions creep into the Church and last for so long?

As I have come to see it, the racial restrictions took on a life of their own after Brigham Young articulated and then defended them. They were not set in stone at his first utterance, nor were they poured down from heaven. The context is earthly, and they grew over time to accumulate historical weight with each succeeding generation unwilling to violate the precedent of the previous generation. Even as late as 1900, President Lorenzo Snow did not consider the restrictions to be settled doctrine. They did harden in place during the opening decade of the twentieth century at the height of

POST-REVELATION JUSTIFICATIONS

racial segregation in the United States, important context to consider.

Yet for some leaders the restrictions remained troubling. Lack of consensus perpetuated the restrictions well into the second half of the twentieth century. They were sustained over time with unsupported assumptions and became so entrenched that it finally took a revelation in 1978 to return the Church to its universal roots and reconcile it with its scriptural mandates that had been there all along.

These historical questions are much easier to answer than the deeper theological questions that the racial restrictions automatically raise. Those questions land at the intersection between my profession and my faith and give me reasons to ponder the weight of this history. I do not believe the racial restrictions were of divine origins. As a historian and a believer, I use the tools of my profession and my faith to navigate what this means to me. My answers may not satisfy everyone, and other believers may arrive at different conclusions. I nonetheless share what I have learned in the chance that it might be useful to others as they grapple with this history. I speak only for myself when doing so.

Absorbing new information can be difficult, and this history is heavy. At times it has felt crushing to me in its enormity. I acknowledge that history is an imprecise discipline and that interpretations can and do change over time, especially when new sources come to light. I have taken time to rearrange my thoughts and to challenge my own prior assumptions precisely because new sources have come to light. The history presented here does in fact include new speeches previously not transcribed from their original shorthand as well as other new evidence only recently uncovered.

Learning new information need not threaten faith. It can instead invite new answers and open new possibilities, especially if we are willing to approach it with an open mind. As President Dieter F. Uchtdorf admonished, "If we stop asking questions, stop thinking, stop pondering, we can thwart the revelations of the Spirit. . . . How often has the Holy Spirit tried to tell us something we needed to know but couldn't get past the massive iron gate of what we thought we already knew?"[2] Letting go of past assumptions can be unsettling, but it can also invite new insights and lift our vision to new heights. For me, the journey has not been easy, and my heart has sometimes broken under the strain of it—and it sometimes still does.

This history is sad to me because I actually believe in the Zion society that is defined in the book of Moses: "And the Lord called his people Zion, because they were of one heart and one mind, and dwelt in righteousness; and there was no poor among them" (Moses 7:18). I also love the vision of unity articulated in the Book of Mormon following the Savior's visit to His people. The Zion society that the former Lamanites and Nephites built was void of "contentions and disputations," and "every man [and woman] did deal justly one with another." In the wake of Christ's visit, His followers "had all things common among them" and "there were not rich and poor, bond and free, but they were all made free, and partakers of the heavenly gift" (4 Nephi 1:2–3).

In fact, "there could not be a happier people among all the people who had been created by the hand of God." They had erased the countless ways that they had invented to divide and hate each other, so much so that "there were no robbers, nor murderers, neither were there Lamanites, nor any manner of -ites; but they were in one, the children of Christ, and heirs to the kingdom of God" (4 Nephi 1:16–17). It is a compelling vision of a godly people, one in which I continue to believe.

Yet, how do we bridge the gap between such lofty ideals and the realities of living in a fallen world? To put it more simply, let me share the question that a deacon in my ward asked me in 2010 when I served as second counselor in the Young Men presidency. The lesson one Sunday was on the attributes of God, and the manual specified that one of those attributes was that God was no respecter of persons. As we

POST-REVELATION JUSTIFICATIONS

discussed this idea, one young man raised his hand and asked, "If God is no respecter of persons, then why did he curse Black people with black skin?"

It is a question that cuts to the heart of the racial restrictions. It is a question that a twelve-year-old boy raised in deacons quorum in 2010 but one that reverberates across time and space. This deacon had grown up in a Church with no racial restrictions but still came to believe that Black people were cursed by God. He rightfully recognized that such an idea conflicted with the very attributes of Godhood. He wanted help to reconcile the contradictions.

This deacon's question highlights the fact that even though the Church lifted its racial restrictions in 1978, it has not actively untaught the falsehoods that sustained the restrictions. They continue to exist among us as Latter-day Saints and are being passed on to the next generation. This is a prime example of the ways in which the sin of racism is multigenerational and became embedded in Latter-day Saint theology, culture, and practice. It underscores the need articulated by President Dallin H. Oaks that as Church members, "we must do better to help root out racism."[3] In the spirit of rooting out racism, here is a list of clarifications that I believe to be true:

- Black people are not now nor were they ever cursed by God.
- Black people are not descendants of Cain, Ham, or Canaan.
- Scriptural curses are not racial impositions; God does not change people's skin color as punishment for sin or reward for repentance.
- Scriptural curses are a separation from God because of sin. Repentance erases the sin and restores God's promised blessings.
- Black people were not neutral, less valiant, evil, or fence-sitters in the premortal realm.
- Black, brown, or any other skin color is not a deterioration

away from whiteness or a sign of a curse or mark placed by God.
- Black people are children of heavenly parents who love all of their children equally.
- White is not somehow the "normal" or default skin color of human beings.
- Black, brown, or any other color of skin will not be white in the Resurrection.
- DNA reveals that we are all a part of the same human family.[4]
- DNA reveals that the entire human population traces its roots to Africa. "Everyone is African," in other words.[5]
- DNA reveals that human beings are genetically more alike than dissimilar, regardless of race or ethnicity. People worldwide carry, on average, 99.9 percent identical DNA.[6]
- Scientists hypothesize that skin color differences are the result of human migrations out of Africa over thousands of years. Skin color adapted to the amount of winter sunlight to which people were exposed. The amount of skin pigmentation in ancestral human populations "is greatest in equatorial Africa and tends to decrease with increased distance from the equator."[7]

At its core, the question from my deacon was an effort to understand where black skin came from. It is based on a faulty premise that white skin is normal and that other skin colors are a deterioration away from white or somehow represent a curse. I believe the racial priesthood and temple restrictions grew out of this same faulty premise. Like others in a fraught nineteenth-century American racial culture, Brigham Young and other Church leaders tried to understand where black skin came from. They assumed that white skin was normal and that black skin then begged an explanation. Biblical marks and curses filled in the gaps in their minds and justified discriminatory policies, teachings, and practices.

Over forty years have passed since the 1978 revelation, and

POST-REVELATION JUSTIFICATIONS

I continue to hear justifications designed to excuse or explain away the restrictions rather than doing the work it takes to root out racism. What follows is a list of the most common justifications in circulation among Latter-day Saints today and why I believe they are incorrect.

Some people have suggested that the Lord spreads the gospel in stages according to a divine timeline: First to the Jews and then to the Gentiles as a parallel to first white people and then to Black people. This justification ignores the fact that Jesus did not confine His ministry to the Jews. He healed the daughter of a Greek woman and testified to a Samaritan woman that He was "the Christ." He then stayed among the Samaritans two days and as a result "many more believed because of his own word." The converted Samaritans soon testified that "this is indeed the Christ, the Saviour of the world" (Mark 7:24–29; John 4:26, 40–42).

As President J. Reuben Clark explained, Jesus taught Peter through example about the gospel's universal message, but it still took "a thrice-repeated vision to convince him that God is no respecter of persons." As President Clark noted, the Savior's "acceptance of the Samaritans, the race hated by Judah, left Peter untaught." Instead of following the Savior's example, he "kicked against the pricks," especially "against the principle of the universal salvation of men—men of all creeds, races, and colors."[8] Peter still resisted even after the Lord commanded His disciples to "go ye into all the world" (Mark 16:15). He thus offers a lesson in how hard it can be for good people, even prophets, to overcome their cultural assumptions and biases, even when the Lord gives them very direct instructions.

In this last dispensation, there was no divinely appointed timeline for spreading the good news of the Restoration. The Lord commanded Joseph Smith five times to preach the gospel "unto every creature." Black Latter-day Saints have been a part of the Church from 1830 to the present, including Black priesthood holders. Suggesting otherwise erases Black pioneers from Latter-day Saint history and wipes away their faith.

The second justification that I sometimes hear is the tribe of Levi example: In the Old Testament, the tribe of Levi was given priesthood authority while members of other tribes were not. The reasoning then offered is that this was a divinely sanctioned pattern that God follows in withholding priesthood from people, first from the non-Levite tribes anciently and then people of African descent in the nineteenth and twentieth centuries.

The tribe of Levi analogy, however, begins with a false premise—that only the tribe of Levi held the priesthood anciently. Book of Mormon peoples were not Levites, and they held the priesthood, as did other Old Testament leaders such as Melchizedek and Elijah.

Even if we confine ourselves to the tribe of Levi's role in the tabernacle, I still believe it is a poor analogy. None of the other tribes were prevented from partaking of the ordinances necessary for their salvation in the way that the temple and priesthood restrictions prevented people of Black African descent from so doing. The tribe of Levi was given authority to administer tabernacle rituals for and in behalf of the other tribes. Their function was to welcome the other tribes into the tabernacle and help them to make their sacrifices as prescribed by the law (see Numbers 3–5). In contrast, the priesthood and temple restrictions prevented Black Latter-day Saints from entering the temple and receiving the ordinances necessary for their salvation. As historian Ardis Parshall succinctly put it, "Restricting priesthood *to* one narrow part of the faithful is not the same as restricting priesthood *from* one narrow part of the faithful."[9]

A third justification in circulation among Latter-day Saints suggests that the racial turbulence of the nineteenth and twentieth centuries was so fraught in the United States that ordaining Black men to the priesthood would have brought down the Church. This idea, however, does not consider the fact that some Black men were given the priesthood in the early decades of the faith and that there was a racially open perspective of temple admission up through Nauvoo. Although it did cause trouble in Missouri and helps to account for the ouster of the Saints from Jackson County, it did not destroy the Church.

This idea suggests that conforming to American racial prejudices was necessary for the Church to survive. However, the same year that Brigham Young openly announced a racial priesthood restriction, 1852, the Church publicly acknowledged that its members believed in and practiced polygamy. Polygamy brought considerable scorn from the nation and did not end until the federal government nearly ground the Church into dust, and yet leaders willfully stood against the crush of derision for what they believed to be a divine principle. It makes me wonder why conforming to racial prejudices would be necessary for the Church to survive but conforming to prevailing marital norms (monogamy) was not necessary.

As Latter-day Saints, we love to quote Joseph Smith's Standard of Truth from the Wentworth Letter, wherein he declares: "The Standard of Truth has been erected; no unhallowed hand can stop the work from progressing; persecutions may rage, mobs may combine, armies may assemble, calumny may defame, but the truth of God will go forth boldly, nobly, and independent, till it has penetrated every continent, visited every clime, swept every country, and sounded in every ear, till the purposes of God shall be accomplished, and the Great Jehovah shall say the work is done."[10] Should we really believe that "no unhallowed hand can stop the work from progressing" and yet treating Black people equally would have?

Fourth, I sometimes hear people suggest that the racial restrictions were merely products of an unenlightened past. Everyone was a racist back then. They did not know any better. We should not impose present-day values on the past, something historians refer to as "presentism." I agree that the past is a foreign country and we should try to understand it on its own terms, not ours, but that is an invitation to do the work of understanding the past, not an invitation to excuse its mistakes as if people in the past somehow did not know any better.

People in the nineteenth century recognized racism as racism by the standards of *their day*. It is a misapplication of presentism and a false use of it to try to justify racism in the past as if no one in the past considered Black people to be anything other than inferior. Enslavers across the North and some in the South, for example, responded to the ideals of the American Revolution to free their slaves. They took Thomas Jefferson at his word when he declared that "all men are created equal" and are "endowed by their Creator with certain unalienable Rights" including "Life, Liberty, and the pursuit of Happiness." After the Revolution, Charles Copland of Virginia freed his enslaved people. He did so, he said, because "God created all men free; & that all Laws made to subjugate one part of the human race to the absolute dominion of another are totally repugnant to the clearest dictates of natural justice."[11]

For Latter-day Saints, Sidney Rigdon was a product of the nineteenth century, and he believed that the nation's founders established a "government where every man should be free; the slave liberated from bondage, and the colored African enjoy the rights of citizenship." In Rigdon's view, the country was founded on principles designed to ensure that all people enjoyed "equal rights to speak, to act, to worship, [with] peculiar privileges to none."[12]

Joseph Smith was also a product of the nineteenth century, and he sanctioned the ordination of Black men to the priesthood. Brigham Young was a product of the nineteenth century, and he called Q. Walker Lewis "one of the best Elders[,] an African." Brigham Young said in 1847, "We don't care about the color," but by 1852, he cared about the color. Apostle Orson Pratt, also a product of the nineteenth century, advocated for Black male voting rights in 1852 in Utah Territory. Brigham Young responded to Pratt's advocacy with a speech filled with racism by the standards of his day.

African Americans, Native Americans, Asian Americans,

POST-REVELATION JUSTIFICATIONS

Latin Americans, and other minority groups also lived in the past and recognized the enslavement and racism they endured as wrong. People in the past were not trapped by historical circumstances outside of their control that somehow made them incapable of rising above their racism. I do not believe that God erased people's agency in the nineteenth century so that they were only capable of treating Black people and other minority groups as inferior. If there were people in the past who argued for full equality for Black people, then it is not an act of presentism to hold people accountable to the standards of *their day*. Racism was racism even in the nineteenth century.

CHAPTER 19

AGENCY AND THE GOSPEL PLAN

"There have been times when members or leaders in the Church have simply made mistakes"

If black skin is not a curse, why did God allow Brigham Young and other leaders to teach that it was? In my estimation, agency lies at the heart of the question. I do not believe God will violate agency, even when we exercise it poorly. The gospel plan is grounded in agency. We fought a war in heaven over it but then sometimes act as if God will revoke our agency in order to save us from our own mistakes. God refuses to violate our agency, even that of prophets. It is the foundation of the plan. If we voted for agency in the premortal realm, then we voted for messiness; when human beings exercise agency it inevitably gets messy.

As Latter-day Saints, we explain the problem of evil with agency. How could loving heavenly parents allow six million of their children to be murdered in the Holocaust or a child to be sexually assaulted or Black people to be enslaved? How could God allow Native Americans to be massacred, wars to ravage nations, and innocent people to die? How can a loving God countenance murder, rape, and the various other unimaginable things God's children do to each other? Agency is so sacred, we answer, that God will not violate it even when we use it to destroy the agency of others.

Yet, we sometimes assume that God would violate Brigham Young's agency when he articulated a cursed racial identity for people of African descent. Orson Pratt never did agree with Brigham Young's racial stance. "We have no proof," he declared, "that the Africans are the descendants of old Cain."[1]

God refused to violate either man's agency. He let them assert their divergent positions regarding race and slavery and then in the long course of the racial restrictions He let those positions harden over time. Because He allows us our agency, however, it does not mean that God approves of our actions. As Elder Ezra Taft Benson taught, God will let us learn things "the hard way." He wants it "to be otherwise, but within certain bounds he grants unto men according to their desires."[2]

Prophets are called of God and possess the keys to administer the ordinances of salvation and to receive revelation. They lead us through the challenges of life and offer wisdom to guide us on our path back to our heavenly parents. They are special witnesses of Jesus Christ and have a divine mandate to point us to salvation through Christ. They teach us about changes we can make to improve who we are as individuals as well as to help us grow as a community of believers. "Repentance," President Nelson recently explained, "is required of every accountable person who desires eternal glory. There are no exceptions."[3]

Our task as followers, the prophet Moroni explains, is to learn from our leaders, even from their mistakes, and use them to become better people. Moroni in fact acknowledged that he and his father had "imperfections" and asked us not to condemn them as a result. Rather, he admonished us to "give thanks unto God that he hath made manifest unto you our imperfections, that ye may learn to be more wise than we have been" (Mormon 9:31). It is a humble request that should resonate in the twenty-first century as a call to learn from the imperfections of our leaders on matters of race and then move forward "more wise" in our resolve to do better.

The wonder of Joseph Smith for me is his willingness to view himself as a "rough stone rolling," to declare himself a prophet and still publicly grapple with his flaws. He printed and published a revelation that announced "how oft" he had "transgressed the commandments and the laws of God, and have gone on in the persuasions of men" (D&C 3:6) and another that declared that he had "not kept the commandments, and must needs stand rebuked before the Lord" (D&C 93:47).

As President Dieter F. Uchtdorf reminded us, "To be perfectly frank, there have been times when members or leaders in the Church have simply made mistakes. There may have been things said or done that were not in harmony with our values, principles, or doctrine." President Uchtdorf continued, "I suppose the Church would be perfect only if it were run by perfect beings. God is perfect, and His doctrine is pure. But He works through us—His imperfect children—and imperfect people make mistakes."[4]

As Latter-day Saints we love certainty, but a gospel plan grounded in agency will inherently contain the uncertainty and messiness of mortality. The plan is certain and its promises are sure even as it offers us choices along the way. Satan's plan, in contrast, offered us certainty without agency and we rejected it. Because we embraced agency, we should expect the messiness that comes with it. As Nephi declared, "For it must needs be, that there is an opposition in all things" (2 Nephi 2:11). Nephi did not say "opposition in all things except Church history."

As Elder Jeffrey R. Holland admonished, "Be kind regarding human frailty—your own as well as that of those who serve with you in a Church led by volunteer, mortal men and women. Except in the case of His only perfect Begotten Son, imperfect people are all God has ever had to work with. That must be terribly frustrating to Him, but He deals with it. So should we. And when you see imperfection, remember that the limitation is not in the divinity of the work."[5]

The Old and New Testaments, the Book of Mormon, and the Doctrine and Covenants are filled with examples of prophets falling short of the divine. God seems to follow a pattern of selecting fallible yet gifted women and men through whom to work. It is not clear to me that He has an alternative. Moses killed an Egyptian and then hid the body in sand. God later spoke to him face to face. Noah was drunk and naked in his tent; Elijah killed 400 of the priests of Baal and then complained when Jezebel sought his life. David committed adultery with Bathsheba and orchestrated Uriah's death to cover his sins. Sariah murmured, Laman and Lemuel rebelled, Judah slept with his daughter-in-law dressed like a harlot, the missionary Corianton left the ministry to chase after a harlot, and the harlot Rahab hid the spies at Jericho and "by faith . . . "perished not" (Hebrews 11:31). Peter denied being a follower of Jesus three times, and Judas, one of the original Twelve Apostles, betrayed Jesus for thirty pieces of silver. The list could go on, but the message seems clear: God is accustomed to working through fallible folks.

With such a track record in prior dispensations, Jesus warned us to expect more of the same as the Restoration began. In His preface to the Doctrine and Covenants He prepared us for the messiness that would follow. The revelations collected up to that point in 1831 were about to be published as a Book of Commandments. He wanted His disciples in the last dispensation to learn from the lessons of the past, that all that God has to work with are imperfect people. He tells the Saints in 1831 that the commandments He has given in the collection of revelations about to be published are from Him: "Behold, I am God and have spoken it; these commandments are of me, and were given unto my servants in their *weakness*, after the manner of their language, that they might come to understanding. And inasmuch as they *erred* it might be made known; And inasmuch as they sought wisdom they might be instructed; And inasmuch as they *sinned* they might be chastened, that they might repent" (D&C 1:24–27; emphasis added).

Jesus Christ Himself saw the "weaknesses" of His servants and predicted their errors and sins. He has a long history of working with weak, error-prone people. His great atoning sacrifice would have been a useless exercise otherwise. If Jesus is willing to accept the weaknesses of His servants, I believe our historical narratives can too.

Jesus goes on to explain in verse 30 that the Church these servants founded is "true and living," speaking unto the Church collectively, not individually. Those two things (being led by weak, error-prone sinners and the Church being collectively true and living) are not mutually exclusive, in other words. Leaders and followers alike have weaknesses, we are prone to error, we will sin, yet collectively—as the body of Christ—we are true and living. Collectively we can bring about much good, including building an inclusive vision of Zion, one in which we are willing to esteem our brothers and sisters as ourselves.

CHAPTER 20

PROPHETIC LEADERSHIP

*"The Lord will never permit me
. . . to lead you astray"*

If the restrictions were wrong, if they were out of harmony with modern and ancient scripture, how do we square them with President Wilford Woodruff's promise that "the Lord will never permit me or any other man who stands as President of this Church to lead you astray"?

It is another challenging question but one that suggests to me that Latter-day Saints sometimes stretch President Woodruff's words beyond their context and intent. President Woodruff was speaking specifically of the 1890 Manifesto, which began the process of ending polygamy. He was defending the Manifesto as a revelation in the face of opposition from some Latter-day Saints who suggested that he was a fallen prophet and was leading the Church astray. His statement, in context, meant that the Lord would not give him a revelation that would lead the Church astray.

His statement is designed to dismiss the accusation that he had merely bowed to political pressure and abandoned polygamy with no authority from God to do so. "It matters not who lives or who dies, or who is called to lead this Church, they have got to lead it by the inspiration of Almighty God," President Woodruff proclaimed in defense of the Manifesto. "If they do not do it that way, they cannot do it at all."[1]

President Woodruff claimed to be leading the Church according to the revelation he received. He told the Latter-day Saints that the Lord had shown him the consequences if the Church entrenched behind polygamy rather than gave it up. The Supreme Court of the United States had decided in May 1890 that Latter-day Saint temples could be confiscated if they were being used for illegal purposes, such as to marry people into polygamy.[2]

Thus, the choice that the Lord showed President Woodruff was between plural marriage and temple worship. As he put it, if the Saints clung to plural marriage, they would do so "at the cost of the confiscation and loss of all the Temples, and the stopping of all the ordinances therein, both for the living and the dead." "The Lord showed me by vision and revelation exactly what would take place if we did not stop this practice," President Woodruff declared.[3] In context, his statement came as an answer to the charge that he was leading the Church astray, something he said he could not do as long as he was acting in accordance with revelation.

CHAPTER 21

JESUS CHRIST IS MIGHTY TO SAVE

"Hath he commanded any that they should not partake of his salvation?"

How do we reconcile what Brigham Young said in 1852, that "this people that [are] commonly called Negros are [the] children of Cain, I know they are; I know they cannot bear rule in [the] priesthood" with the fact that Jesus Christ twice declared in 1831, "I am no respecter of persons" (D&C 1:35; 38:16)? There are no easy answers that will satisfy everyone, but in my estimation, our faith is stronger for having wrestled with such questions.

In 1897, Elder Joseph F. Smith articulated a view that seems applicable. Elder Smith was speaking of Brigham Young's idea that Adam was the God of this world, a teaching sometimes referred to as the "Adam-God theory." It was something that Brigham Young taught repeatedly but that did not mesh with scriptural understandings and was eventually denounced as "false doctrine."[1] Joseph F. Smith explained, "While I am not authorized to sit in judgment upon Pres[iden]t Young, I am at liberty to test the truth of his words or utterances by the revealed and accepted word of God. Anything uttered by man which is contrary to the Divine law must fall, while that only which is in harmony with it can remain, or stand."[2]

Were the Church's teachings on race in harmony with "the revealed and accepted word of God"? Nephi asked in the Book of Mormon, "Hath [God] commanded any that they should depart out of the synagogues, or out of the houses of worship? Behold, I say unto you, Nay. Hath he commanded any that they should not partake of his salvation? Behold I say unto you, Nay" (2 Nephi 26:26–27). The racial priesthood and temple restrictions, however, did just that. They prevented people of African descent from partaking of Christ's salvation and denied them access to the "houses of worship" where the highest ordinances of their faith were performed.

I value being a part of a religious tradition that is led by a prophet, especially as that prophet does the difficult work of leading a worldwide ministry that asks him to align his will with the will of the Savior. Ultimately, however, prophets are human, and their role is to point their followers toward the divine. As Terryl and Fiona Givens have reminded us, "God specifically said that He called weak vessels so we wouldn't place our faith in their strength or power, but in God's."[3] Only Jesus Christ is "mighty to save" (D&C 133:47). We do not need an infallible prophet when we have an infallible Savior.

As Latter-day Saints we believe in eternal progression, a beautiful doctrine that might help us to situate Brigham Young in a longer-term perspective than his views from 1852 allow.[4] In an eternal perspective, Brigham Young is not in some corner of the eternities stuck on his racial position from 1852. I believe that he has had plenty of time to progress, and we can too. "We condemn racism," the Church declared in 2012, "including any and all past racism by individuals both inside and outside the Church."[5] Rather than deny or defend the racism, what if we were willing to acknowledge its ugliness and to collectively lift its weight?

Church leaders have set an example in recent years and begun to model the possibilities. In family history work the Church has made a lasting commitment to digitize and index Freedmen's Bank and Bureau records, a boon in attempting to trace formerly enslaved people over time. The Freedmen's Bank and Bureau was an important post–Civil War government entity designed to offer formerly enslaved people banking and other services. The freed people who registered with the bureau were therefore recorded in its documents by name, sometimes for the first time in their lives, making it a unique family history resource for African Americans.[6]

In 2019, the Church also announced a $2 million donation to the International African American Museum at the former Gadsden's Wharf in Charleston, South Carolina. Gadsden's Wharf is the site where more enslaved Africans landed in slave ships than any other place in the United States. The Church's contribution was aimed at creating a Center for Family History at the new museum in an effort to help African Americans trace their ancestral roots, which were so profoundly torn apart by slavery.[7]

In addition to its family history efforts, the Church began a relationship with the National Association for the Advancement of Colored People in 2018, which has continued to develop over time. That partnership fostered a joint national opinion piece between President Nelson and NAACP leaders. Together they called for the "wheels of justice" to "move fairly for all" and noted that "Jesus of Nazareth came that we might have life, and have it 'more abundantly.' We should follow His example and seek for an abundant life for all God's children." The joint statement invited "people of goodwill everywhere to look for ways to reach out and serve someone of a different background or race. Everyone can do something." NAACP leaders and President Nelson, however, went even further to recognize that racism goes well beyond individual feelings and attitudes, especially in the ways it has become embedded in the nation's systems and laws. They therefore called on "government, business, and educational leaders at every level to review processes, laws, and organizational attitudes regarding racism and root them out once and for all."[8]

Recognizing that racism exists among us as Latter-day Saints, leaders have additionally sounded a steady drumbeat in their calls for repentance. President Gordon B. Hinckley indicated that no person "who makes disparaging remarks concerning those of another race can consider himself a true disciple of Christ."[9] President M. Russell Ballard admonished us to "embrace God's children compassionately and eliminate any prejudice, including racism, sexism, and nationalism."[10]

LET'S TALK ABOUT RACE AND PRIESTHOOD

President Dallin H. Oaks called the phrase *Black lives matter* "an eternal truth all reasonable people should support" and described racism as "not consistent with the revealed word of God." He went on to "condemn racism by any group toward any other group worldwide."[11] And President Nelson grieved "that our Black brothers and sisters the world over are enduring the pains of racism and prejudice" and called on Latter-day Saints to be at the forefront of change.[12]

CHAPTER 22

A PATH FORWARD

*"Lead out in abandoning attitudes
and actions of prejudice"*

How can Latter-day Saints in the twenty-first century heed President Nelson's call to "members everywhere to lead out in abandoning attitudes and actions of prejudice"? President Nelson pled with us "to promote respect for all of God's children."[1] How do we answer his call if we are unable to recognize what prejudice looks like among us? How do we "root out racism" if we are unwilling to examine its roots? History can help us to learn from the past in order to create a more respectful future.[2]

President Nelson has called us to action. It is a process that requires self-reflection, honesty, repentance, and a willingness to abandon prior justifications that led us to treat our Black brothers and sisters as cursed and inferior. Equipped with an understanding of the past, each of us now becomes accountable in the present for our attitudes and actions as well as an agent of change for the future.

It is much more profitable, in my estimation, to learn from our collective history rather than defend or deny it. What lessons can it teach? Latter-day Saints experienced racialization at the hands of outsiders, and Latter-day Saints engaged in racism on the inside. What better people to lead out on issues of racial inequality and social justice? Rather than be hobbled by our past racism, what if we owned it and used our shared history to stand in places of empathy? What if we were willing to work against racial injustice because we experienced a soft form of it? What if we were willing to speak up and stand up against systemic racism because we engaged in it ourselves and have come to understand its consequences? What if we were willing, like Jesus, to claim "all flesh" as our own?[3]

In a revelation to Joseph Smith in 1831, Jesus Christ offers us a way to do just that: "And let every man esteem his brother as himself, and practice virtue and holiness before me," He admonishes (D&C 38:24). That is my calling as a disciple of Christ: to esteem my brothers and sisters as myself. However, if we imagine our brothers and sisters to be only people who look like us, we are missing the point. To esteem our brothers and sisters as ourselves is a call to recognize the diversity that exists among us, to see color and do the work that it takes to understand what life looks like from someone else's perspective.

Jane Manning James was repeatedly denied temple admission and Freda Beaulieu waited over sixty-nine years to enter a temple—am I willing to esteem their experiences as my own? Elijah Able was denied his endowment and the chance to be sealed to his wife—am I willing to claim his flesh as my own? Marie Graves was denied access to Sunday worship services because she was Black—am I willing to walk a mile in her shoes? Am I willing to esteem these brothers and sisters as myself and recognize that because the color of my skin is lighter than theirs, I may experience life differently than they do? Am I willing to listen to their experiences and "practice virtue and holiness" rather than become defensive?

In verse 26, Jesus emphasizes His point. He wants us to understand what He means when He tells us He is no respecter of persons: "For what man among you having twelve sons, and is no respecter of them, and they serve him obediently, and he saith unto the one: Be thou clothed in robes and sit thou here; and to the other: Be thou clothed in rags and sit thou there—and looketh upon his sons and saith I am just?" (D&C 38:26).

If we slightly modify that verse, we can make it applicable to the racial restrictions of the past and the racism of the present: "For what man among you having twelve sons, and is no respecter of them, and they serve him obediently, and he saith unto the one: Be thou ordained to the priesthood and sit thou here; and to the other: Be thou cursed for a murder in which you took no part and thus barred from the priesthood and temple and sit thou there—and looketh upon his sons and saith I am just?"

As the prophet Jacob asserts, pride leads us to "persecute [our] brethren because [we] suppose that [we] are better than they" (Jacob 2:13). But in God's eyes, "one being is as precious . . . as the other." In case that idea is not convincing enough, Jacob reminds us of our ultimate fate: "All flesh is of the dust," he flatly declares (Jacob 2:21). Regardless of what our particular color of flesh might be, we will all return to dust, and then how superior will we be? Jacob asks us to "remember [our] own filthiness" before we "revile against" anyone else "because of the darkness of their skins" (Jacob 3:8–9). He thus offers a deeply insightful formula for abandoning attitudes and actions of prejudice, one that Latter-day Saints might consider as we load our handcarts with the weight of our racial past and begin to pull them toward Zion.

In 1874, the formerly enslaved man Samuel Chambers served in the office of deacon in the Salt Lake Eighth Ward, even though he was not ordained. His vision of a Zion society was one of unity and inclusion amid diversity, a model for the twenty-first century. He reminded his fellow deacons that the gospel "is not only to the Gentiles but also to the African, for I am of that race. The knowledge I received is from God," he declared. "I pray that we may be as one to build up the Kingdom of God," he pled in a supplication that reverberates to the present and invites us all to join him in the work of inclusion.[4]

FURTHER READING

General Histories

Harris, Matthew L., and Newell G. Bringhurst. *The Mormon Church and Blacks: A Documentary History.* Urbana: University of Illinois Press, 2015.

Mauss, Armand L. *All Abraham's Children: Changing Mormon Conceptions of Race and Lineage.* Urbana: University of Illinois Press, 2003.

Newell, Quincy D. *Your Sister in the Gospel: The Life of Jane Manning James, A Nineteenth-Century Black Mormon.* New York: Oxford University Press, 2019.

Reeve, W. Paul. *Religion of a Different Color: Race and the Mormon Struggle for Whiteness.* New York: Oxford University Press, 2015.

Reeve, W. Paul, Christopher B. Rich Jr., and LaJean Purcell Carruth. *This Abominable Slavery: Race, Religion, and the Battle over Human Bondage in Antebellum Utah.* New York: Oxford University Press.

Stevenson, Russell W. *For the Cause of Righteousness: A Global History of Blacks and Mormonism, 1830–2013.* Salt Lake City: Greg Kofford Books, 2014.

Thiriot, Amy Tanner. *Slaves in Zion: African American Servitude in Utah Territory.* Salt Lake City: University of Utah Press, 2022.

Journal Articles

Bush Jr., Lester E. "Mormonism's Negro Doctrine: An Historical Overview," *Dialogue: A Journal of Mormon Thought* 8 (Spring 1973): 11–68.

Jones, Christopher C. "'A very poor place for our doctrine': Religion and Race in the 1853 Mormon Mission to Jamaica." *Religion and American Culture: A Journal of Interpretation* 31 (Summer 2021): 262–95.

FURTHER READING

Kimball, Edward L. "Spencer W. Kimball and the Revelation on Priesthood." *BYU Studies* 47, no. 2 (2008): 5–78.

Reeve, W. Paul. "'I Dug the Graves': Isaac Lewis Manning, Joseph Smith, and Racial Connections in Two Latter-day Saint Traditions." *Journal of Mormon History* 47 (January 2021): 29–67.

Talmage, Jeremy, and Clinton D. Christensen. "Black, White, or Brown? Racial Perceptions and the Priesthood Policy in Latin America." *Journal of Mormon History* 44 (January 2018): 119–45.

Websites

Century of Black Mormons, http://centuryofblackmormons.org.

"Race and the Priesthood," Gospel Topics Essays, The Church of Jesus Christ of Latter-day Saints, https://www.ChurchofJesusChrist.org/study/manual/gospel-topics-essays/race-and-the-priesthood?lang=eng.

ACKNOWLEDGMENTS

I have accumulated a number of debts in the process of crafting this manuscript. Several friends read drafts and offered feedback that strengthened the end result. Tyler Johnson, Scott Woodward, Peter Bennion, Matthew Grow, J. B. Haws, Ben Spackman, Ronell Hugh, Morgan Davis, and Mauli Bonner all shared their wisdom and insight with me. Jonathan Stapley and Ardis Parshall not only read drafts, offered sources, and suggested edits; they also became an essential sounding board and support team. I will forever cherish their encouragement.

Janae and Cris Baird, Kristine Wright, Steven Snow, Marlin Jensen, Briant Carter, Patrick Mason, Thomas Griffith, Margaret Blair Young, Dalyn and Kay Montgomery, Mable Burt, Herb Riggs, Jeff Turner, Leigh Odimah, Madeline Hale, Lola Ogunbote, Charlotte Steinfeld, Naomi Notice, Zinta Jaunitis, Karyn Dudley, Tony and Dorothy Perkins, Sheryl and Matt Garner, Heather and Greg McMurray, Ron and Cheri Campbell, Robert and Alice Burch, and Jim and Ema Anderson offered inspiration and boosts when I needed them most, even without necessarily knowing about this project.

LaJean Purcell Carruth transcribed the Brigham Young and Orson Pratt speeches quoted here, and Christopher Rich helped to analyze them and situate them within their nineteenth-century contexts. Thank you both for such important work.

Darius Gray was my companion and confidant on this journey and my trusted advisor. Calling him friend and brother is one of the honors of my life. To have his foreword at the beginning of this book is a treasure all its own. Thank you, dear friend. Your example continues to inspire me.

I admire the vision of my friends at Deseret Book

ACKNOWLEDGMENTS

publishing in bringing this book into existence and honor their dedication to its message.

My mom and brother were fans of this project from the beginning and offered reassurances (and impatience (Mom)) along the way. Their confidence sustained me.

My children checked in on the status of the book too and always had a word or two of advice to proffer whether I wanted it or not. Porter, Eliza, Josh, Rebecca, Emma, and Hunter, you give me hope for a better future.

Finally, Beth, there is no one I'd rather share life's journey with than you. Thank you for holding my hand as we stumble along together.

NOTES

Abbreviations

The following abbreviations are used in the notes:

BYU   L. Tom Perry Special Collections, Harold B. Lee Library, Brigham Young University, Provo, Utah.

CBM   *Century of Black Mormons*, http://centuryofblackmormons.org.

CHL   Church History Library, The Church of Jesus Christ of Latter-day Saints, Salt Lake City, Utah.

D&C   Doctrine and Covenants.

JD   *Journal of Discourses*, 26 vols. (Liverpool: F. D. and S. W. Richards, 1855–86).

JWML   Special Collections, J. Willard Marriot Library, University of Utah, Salt Lake City, Utah.

RDC   W. Paul Reeve, *Religion of a Different Color: Race and the Mormon Struggle for Whiteness* (New York: Oxford University Press, 2015).

WWJ   *The Wilford Woodruff Journals*, typescript, 6 vols., edited by Dan Vogel (Salt Lake City, Utah: Benchmark Books, 2020).

Foreword

1. Gospel Topics, "Race and the Priesthood," topics.ChurchofJesus Christ.org.

Introduction

1. W. Paul Reeve, "Nelson Holder Ritchie," *CBM,* https://exhibits.lib.utah.edu/s/century-of-black-mormons/page/ritchie-nelson-holder.
2. John Mills Whitaker, Memorandum from the daily journal of John M. Whitaker (December 1906 to March 1912), typescript of transcripts from John M. Whitaker journal, 150, JWML.
3. William C. Mann, mission journal, MS 26229, 99–100, CHL.
4. Whitaker, Memorandum, 150.
5. Whitaker, Memorandum, 150.
6. Russell M. Nelson, "Let God Prevail," *Ensign*, November 2020.
7. Reeve, "Nelson Holder Ritchie."
8. Devery S. Anderson, ed., *The Development of LDS Temple Worship, 1846–2000: A Documentary History* (Salt Lake City: Signature Books, 2011), 82, 101–2, 361.
9. Reeve, "Nelson Holder Ritchie."
10. Reeve, "Nelson Holder Ritchie."

NOTES

11. W. Paul Reeve, "Russell Dewey Ritchie," *CBM*, https://exhibits.lib.utah.edu/s/century-of-black-mormons/page/ritchie-russell-dewey.
12. Reeve, "Russell Dewey Ritchie."
13. The Church of Jesus Christ of Latter-day Saints, Record of Members Collection, Holly Park Ward, CR 375 8, CHL; Reeve, "Russell Dewey Ritchie."
14. Reeve, "Russell Dewey Ritchie."
15. Reeve, "Nelson Holder Ritchie."
16. For the Latter-day Saint racial story within a broader national context, see W. Paul Reeve, *Religion of a Different Color: Race and the Mormon Struggle for Whiteness* (New York: Oxford University Press, 2015).
17. Nelson, "Let God Prevail."
18. "Report from the Presidency," *Times and Seasons* (Nauvoo, Illinois), October 1840, 188.

Chapter 1: Black Converts in the U.S. North

1. Matt McBride, "Peter," *CBM*, https://exhibits.lib.utah.edu/s/century-of-black-mormons/page/peter; Mark L. Staker, *Hearken, O Ye People: The Historical Setting of Joseph Smith's Ohio Revelations* (Salt Lake City, Utah: Greg Kofford Books, 2009), 5–91.
2. Gospel Topics, "Race and the Priesthood," topics.ChurchofJesusChrist.org.
3. See W. Paul Reeve, "Elijah Able," "Moroni Able," and "Elijah R. Ables" at *CBM*; W. Paul Reeve, "Elijah Able," *CBM*, https://exhibits.lib.utah.edu/s/century-of-black-mormons/page/able-elijah; Russell W. Stevenson, "'A Negro Preacher': The Worlds of Elijah Ables," *Journal of Mormon History* 39 (Spring 2013): 171.
4. United States, 1850 Census, Ohio, Cincinnati, Hamilton; United States, 1860 Census, Utah Territory, Salt Lake County, Salt Lake City, 13th Ward; United States, 1870 Census, Utah Territory, Weber County, Ogden; United States, 1880 Census, Utah Territory, Salt Lake County, Salt Lake City 8th Ward.
5. Utah, Salt Lake County Death Records, 1849–1949, Elijah Able.
6. Joseph F. Smith, Notes on Elijah Able, undated [likely ca. 1879], Joseph F. Smith Papers, CHL.
7. Kirtland elders' certificates, 1836–1838, CR 100 401, folder 1, image 83, CHL.
8. H. Michael Marquardt, ed., Early Patriarchal Blessings of The Church of Jesus Christ of Latter-day Saints (Salt Lake City: Smith-Pettit Foundation, 2007), 99.
9. Joseph F. Smith, Notes on Elijah Able. Joseph F. Smith's handwritten record specifies "Judge Beaman & Reuben P. Hadlock" as the men who performed Able's washing and anointing ritual. Alvah Beman was the president of the elders quorum in Kirtland and Ruben Hedlock was his counselor—certainly the people to whom the document refers.
10. Seventies Record Book A, CR 3 51, CHL.

NOTES

11. Eunice Kinney, letter to Wingfield Watson, September 1891, BYU.
12. Historian's Office Minutes and Reports (local units), 1840–1886, Ohio, 1843–1844, CR 100 589, images 3–7, CHL.
13. Jordan T. Watkins, "Quack Walker Lewis," *CBM*, https://exhibits.lib.utah.edu/s/century-of-black-mormons/page/lewis-quack-walker.
14. Wilford Woodruff to Brigham Young, November 16, 1844, Brigham Young office files, CR 1234 1, CHL.
15. Watkins, "Quack Walker Lewis."
16. Trustee-in-Trust tithing and donation record, May 1844–January 1846, CR 5 85, 302–3, 431, 573, 692, CHL; Watkins, "Quack Walker Lewis."
17. W. Paul Reeve, "'I Dug the Graves': Isaac Lewis Manning, Joseph Smith, and Racial Connections in Two Latter-day Saint Traditions," *Journal of Mormon History* 47 (January 2021): 43–46.
18. Philadelphia Branch Record Book, MS 8457, 22–25, CHL; Reeve, "I Dug the Graves," 43–46.
19. William G. Hartley, "From Men to Boys: LDS Aaronic Priesthood Offices, 1829–1996," *Journal of Mormon History* 22 (Spring 1996): 80–136.
20. Jane Manning James, "Jane Manning James Autobiography" (ca. 1902), folio 1 recto, MS 4425, CHL; Quincy D. Newell, *Your Sister in the Gospel: The Life of Jane Manning James, A Nineteenth-Century Black Mormon* (New York: Oxford University Press, 2019), 20–22. See also James's autobiography as reproduced in Newell, *Your Sister in the Gospel,* appendix, 144. Future references to the autobiography will be to the Newell version.
21. James, Autobiography, 149; Reeve, "I Dug the Graves," 30.
22. Reeve, "I Dug the Graves," 29–37.
23. The Book of the Law of the Lord, 1840–1846, MS 22507, 309–10, CHL.
24. Reeve, "I Dug the Graves," 36–39.
25. James, Autobiography, 144.
26. James, Autobiography, 145; Susa Young Gates, compiler and editor, "Joseph Smith, the Prophet," *Young Woman's Journal* 16, no. 12 (December 1905): 551–53.
27. "Was Cook for Prophet Joseph; Negro at Pioneer Day Fete," *Salt Lake Herald Republican*, July 26, 1910, 10.
28. "First Negroes to Join Mormon Church," *Salt Lake Herald*, October 2, 1899, 5; Reeve, "I Dug the Graves," 66.
29. Gates, "Joseph Smith, the Prophet."
30. "Died," *Saints' Herald* (Plano, IL), January 4, 1890.
31. E. J. D. Roundy, "Communicated," *Deseret Evening News*, April 17, 1911, 3; Reeve, "I Dug the Graves," 40.
32. James, Autobiography, 147.
33. Reeve, "I Dug the Graves," 47–50.
34. Isaac L. Manning statement, November 6, 1903, MS 3974, CHL.

NOTES
Chapter 2: Black Converts in the U.S. South

1. W. Paul Reeve, "John Burton," *CBM,* https://exhibits.lib.utah.edu/s/century-of-black-mormons/page/burton-john.
2. Trustee-in-Trust, Tithing Daybooks, Daybook C, CR 5 71, CHL.
3. Joseph Lee Robinson Papers, Autobiography, MS 7042, 47, CHL.
4. Joseph Lee Robinson Papers, Autobiography, 67, 76–77.
5. Richard E. Bennett, *Mormons at the Missouri: Winter Quarters, 1846–1852* (Norman: University of Oklahoma Press, 1987), chapter 7.
6. Joseph Lee Robinson Papers, Records, 1846–1847, MS 7042, reel 1, folder 4, CHL.
7. The Church of Jesus Christ of Latter-day Saints, Record of Members Collection, Parowan Ward, CR 375 8, CHL; Reeve, "John Burton."
8. Rance Hutchings research notes, in Donald E. Burton, History of John Burton, 1797–1865, typescript, MS 21263, 25, CHL.
9. David W. Blight, *Frederick Douglass: Prophet of Freedom* (New York: Simon and Schuster, 2018), 13.
10. Reeve, "John Burton."
11. Ami Chopine, "Lewis Copeland," *CBM,* https://exhibits.lib.utah.edu/s/century-of-black-mormons/page/copeland-lewis; Ami Chopine, "Robert Copeland," *CBM,* https://exhibits.lib.utah.edu/s/century-of-black-mormons/page/copeland-robert; Ami Chopine, "Jack," *CBM,* https://exhibits.lib.utah.edu/s/century-of-black-mormons/page/jack.
12. Chopine, "Lewis Copeland"; Chopine, "Robert Copeland."
13. Summary of interview with Mrs. Rose Brown Hayes and Mrs. Clark, February 1, 1936, MSS 1581, BYU; Julia Huddleston, "Betsy Brown Fluellen," *CBM,* https://exhibits.lib.utah.edu/s/century-of-black-mormons/page/fluellen-betsy-brown.
14. Leonard J. Arrington, Feramorz Y. Fox, and Dean L. May, *Building the City of God: Community and Cooperation among the Mormons*, second edition (Urbana and Chicago: University of Illinois Press, 1992), chapter 4.
15. John Brown, Consecration Deed, MSS 3905, 81–82, BYU; Huddleston, "Betsy Brown Fluellen."
16. The Church of Jesus Christ of Latter-day Saints, Record of Members Collection, Lehi Ward, CR 375 8, images 117–18, CHL; Huddleston, "Betsy Brown Fluellen."
17. Huddleston, "Betsy Brown Fluellen."
18. [William G. Hartley], "Saint Without Priesthood," *Dialogue: A Journal of Mormon Thought* 12, no. 2 (Summer 1979): 17.
19. [Hartley], "Saint Without Priesthood," 18.
20. Tonya Reiter, "Life on the Hill: The Black Farming Families of Mill Creek," *Journal of Mormon History* 44 (October 2018): 68–89.
21. [Hartley], "Saint Without Priesthood," 13–16.
22. [Hartley], "Saint Without Priesthood," 16–18.
23. [Hartley], "Saint Without Priesthood," 17, 18, 20–21.
24. [Hartley], "Saint Without Priesthood," 18.

NOTES

Chapter 3: Race Relations in Jackson County, Missouri

1. W. W. Phelps, "Free People of Color," *The Evening and the Morning Star*, July 1833; *RDC*, 116–121.
2. Theda Perdue and Michael D. Green, eds., *The Cherokee Removal: A Brief History with Documents*, 2nd ed. (Boston: Bedford/St. Martin's, 2005), 127–28.
3. Edmund S. Morgan, *American Slavery, American Freedom: The Ordeal of Colonial Virginia* (New York: W. W. Norton & Company, 1975).
4. Marika Sherwood, *After Abolition: Britain and the Slave Trade Since 1807* (London: I.B. Tauris, 2007).
5. Manisha Sinha, *The Slave's Cause: A History of Abolition* (New Haven, CT: Yale University Press, 2016), chapter 3.
6. *RDC*, introduction.
7. Reginal Horsman, *Race and Manifest Destiny: The Origins of American Racial Anglo-Saxonism* (Cambridge, MA: Harvard University Press, 1981).
8. "An Act to Establish an Uniform Rule of Naturalization," 1st Cong., 26 March 1790, Sess. II, chap. 3, 1 stat 103.
9. *Congressional Globe,* 30th Cong., 1st Sess. (Washington, DC: Blair and Rives, 1848), 98.
10. *Scott v. Sandford,* 60 US 393, p. 407.
11. Thomas Jefferson, *Notes on the State of Virginia* (Richmond, VA: J. W. Randolph, 1853), 155.
12. P. J. Staudenraus, *The African Colonization Movement, 1816–1865* (New York: Columbia University Press, 1961).
13. Eric Foner, *The Fiery Trial: Abraham Lincoln and American Slavery* (New York: W. W. Norton, 2010).
14. Henry Mayer, *All on Fire: William Lloyd Garrison and the Abolition of Slavery* (New York: St. Martin's Press, 1998); *RDC*, 115–16.
15. Elise Lemire, *"Miscegenation": Making Race in America* (Philadelphia: University of Pennsylvania Press, 2002); *RDC*, 116.
16. Phelps, "Free People of Color."
17. Phelps, "Free People of Color"; *RDC*, 118.
18. Phelps, "Free People of Color."
19. W. W. Phelps, *The Evening and the Morning Star Extra,* July 16, 1833; *RDC*, 118.
20. *RDC*, 118–20.
21. "Regulating the Mormonites," *Erie Gazette* (Erie, PA), September 5, 1833.
22. "To His Excellency, Daniel Dunklin, Governor of the State of Missouri," *The Evening and the Morning Star* (Kirtland, OH), December 1833.
23. E. S. Abdy, *Journal of a Residence and Tour in the United States of North America,* 3 vols. (London: John Murray, 1835), 3:41–42.
24. *RDC*, 120–22.

NOTES

Chapter 4: Outsiders View the Latter-day Saints Racially

1. *RDC*, chapter 1.
2. "To His Excellency, Daniel Dunklin, Governor of the State of Missouri," *The Evening and the Morning Star* (Kirtland, OH), December 1883.
3. Alexander Majors, *Seventy Years on the Frontier: Alexander Majors' Memoirs of a Lifetime on the Border*, ed. Prentiss Ingraham (Chicago: Rand McNally, 1893; repr., Lincoln: University of Nebraska Press, 1989), 45.
4. Parley P. Pratt, *Late Persecution of the Church of Jesus Christ of Latter-day Saints* (New York: J. W. Harrison, 1840), 59; *RDC*, 22.
5. "Conference Minutes," *Times and Seasons*, November 1, 1845, 1012; RDC, 24.
6. David J. Whittaker, "The Bone in the Throat: Orson Pratt and the Public Announcement of Plural Marriage," *Western Historical Quarterly* 18 (July 1987): 293–314.
7. *RDC*, chapters 1–3.
8. *RDC*, 24–43.
9. US Senate, *Statistical Report on the Sickness and Morality in the Army of the United States,* Senate Executive Document 52, 36th Cong., 1st Sess., 301–2.
10. US Senate, *Statistical Report*, 301–2.
11. *Reynolds v. United States* (1879), 98 US 153, 161–68; *RDC*, 240.
12. "The Census Uncertainties," *St. Louis Globe Democrat* (St. Louis, Missouri), January 30, 1883; *RDC*, 185.
13. Ariela J. Gross, *What Blood Won't Tell: A History of Race on Trial in America* (Cambridge, Massachusetts: Harvard University Press, 2008), 138–39.

Chapter 5: Latter-day Saints and Slavery in the 1830s and '40s

1. *RDC*, chapter 4.
2. Larry E. Tise, *Proslavery: A History of the Defense of Slavery in America, 1701–1840* (Athens: University of Georgia Press, 1987), 267–68; Brycchan Carey and Geoffrey Plank, eds., *Quakers and Abolition* (Urbana: University of Illinois Press, 2014), 1–12, 43–55; *RDC*, 122.
3. The declaration was first published in the *Latter Day Saints' Messenger and Advocate* (Kirtland, OH), August 1835, under the heading "General Assembly"; it was also included as Section 102 in "Doctrine and Covenants, 1835," 252–54, The Joseph Smith Papers, accessed September 22, 2020, https://www.josephsmithpapers.org/paper-summary/doctrine-and-covenants-1835/262, and eventually became Section 134 in more recent versions of the Doctrine and Covenants.
4. Joseph Smith Jr., "For the Messenger and Advocate," *Latter Day Saints' Messenger and Advocate* (Kirtland, OH), April 1836.

NOTES

5. Smith, "For the Messenger and Advocate."
6. David M. Goldenberg, *The Curse of Ham: Race and Slavery in Early Judaism, Christianity, and Islam* (Princeton, NJ: Princeton University Press, 2003), 1.
7. Smith, "For the Messenger and Advocate."
8. Smith, "For the Messenger and Advocate."
9. *Elders' Journal* (Far West, Caldwell Co., MO), July 1838, 43.
10. Newell G. Bringhurst, *Saints, Slaves, and Blacks: The Changing Place of Black People within Mormonism,* 2nd edition (Salt Lake City: Greg Kofford Books, 2018), 52–56; Leonard L. Richards, *"Gentlemen of Property and Standing": Anti-Abolition Mobs in Jacksonian America* (New York: Oxford University Press, 1970), 156–70.
11. *RDC*, chapter 4.
12. In *The Joseph Smith Papers, Journals, Volume 2: December 1841–April 1843*, ed. Andrew H. Hedges, Alex D. Smith, and Richard Lloyd Anderson, (Salt Lake City, UT: Church Historian's Press, 2011), 212.
13. In *The Joseph Smith Papers, Journals, Volume 2: December 1841–April 1843*, 212.
14. Joseph Smith, *General Smith's Views of the Powers and Policy of the Government of the United States*, Nauvoo, Illinois, 7 February 1844.
15. Smith, *General Smith's Views,* 9.
16. Smith, *General Smith's Views,* 9, 11.
17. Smith, *General Smith's Views*, 3.
18. Smith, *General Smith's Views*, 3.
19. Smith, *General Smith's Views*, 3–4.
20. In *Council of Fifty, Minutes*, ed. Matthew J. Grow, Ronald K. Esplin, Mark Ashurst-McGee, Jeffrey D. Mahas, Matthew C. Godfrey, Gerrit J. Dirkmaat (Salt Lake City, UT: Church Historian's Press, September 2016), 111–13.
21. C. C. Goen, *Broken Churches, Broken Nation: Denominational Schisms and the Coming of the American Civil War* (Macon, GA: Mercer University Press, 1985).
22. W. Paul Reeve, Christopher B. Rich Jr., and LaJean Purcell Carruth, *This Abominable Slavery: Race, Religion, and the Battle over Human Bondage in Antebellum Utah* (New York: Oxford University Press), chapters 2–3.

Chapter 6: Universalism at Nauvoo

1. "Report from the Presidency," *Times and Seasons* (Nauvoo, Illinois), October 1840, 188.
2. Heber C. Kimball, Journal, October 14, 1845, MS 652, JWML; *RDC*, 81.
3. W. Paul Reeve, "Sarah Ann Mode Hofheintz," *CBM*, https://exhibits.lib.utah.edu/s/century-of-black-mormons/page/hofheintz-sarah-ann-mode.
4. Reeve, "Sarah Ann Mode Hofheintz."
5. Reeve, "Sarah Ann Mode Hofheintz."

NOTES

Chapter 7: Race at Winter Quarters

1. Angela Pulley Hudson, *Real Native Genius: How an Ex-Slave and a White Mormon became Famous Indians* (Chapel Hill: University of North Carolina Press, 2015), 38–42, 65–68; *RDC*, 128–29.
2. *WWJ*, February 26, 1847, 2:176.
3. Charles Kelly, ed., *Journal of John D. Lee, 1846–47 and 1859* (Salt Lake City, UT: privately printed for Western Printing Company, 1938), 100.
4. *WWJ*, March 26, 1847, 2:179.
5. Kelly, *Journal of John D. Lee*, 103.
6. The journal of Lorenzo Brown, April 25, 1847, 10, CHL.
7. Juanita Brooks, ed., *On the Mormon Frontier: The Diary of Hosea Stout, 1844–1861*, vol. 1 (Salt Lake City: University of Utah Press and Utah State Historical Society, 1964), 304.
8. Nelson W. Whipple, autobiography and journal, MS 9995, 30, CHL.
9. Brooks, *On the Mormon Frontier*, 244.
10. Church Historian's Office, General Church Minutes, 1839–1877, CR 100 318, March 26, 1847, CHL; *RDC*, 130.
11. General Church Minutes, March 26, 1847; *RDC*, 130–31.
12. General Church Minutes, March 26, 1847; *RDC*, 132.

Chapter 8: Old Testament Curses and the Book of Abraham

1. General Church Minutes, 1839–1877, CR 100 318, April 25, 1847, CHL; *RDC*, 133.
2. "The Book of Abraham," *Times and Seasons*, March 1, 1842, 705.
3. Richard Lyman Bushman, *Joseph Smith, Rough Stone Rolling: A Cultural Biography of Mormonism's Founder* (New York: Alfred A. Knopf, 2005), 285–89; Irene Bates and E. Gary Smith, *Lost Legacy: The Mormon Office of Presiding Patriarch* (Urbana: University of Illinois Press, 1996).
4. Terryl Givens with Brian M. Hauglid, *The Pearl of Greatest Price: Mormonism's Most Controversial Scripture* (New York: Oxford University Press, 2019), 131–37; Matthew L. Harris and Newell G. Bringhurst, *The Mormon Church and Blacks: A Documentary History* (Urbana: University of Illinois Press, 2015), 12–13.
5. *RDC*, chapter 5, 205–8; Givens and Hauglid, *The Pearl of Greatest Price*, 1–22.
6. This explanation of Old Testament curses is drawn from Ben Spackman, "Come Follow Me: 2 Nephi 1–2," February 8, 2020, https://benspackman.com/2020/02/bom-gospel-doctrine-lesson-6-2-nephi-1-2/#more-1573 and Ben Spackman, "Old Testament Gospel Doctrine Lesson 17: Deuteronomy," July 2, 2018, https://benspackman.com/2018/07/gospel-doctrine-17-deuteronomy/.
7. Diedre Nicole Green, *Jacob, A Brief Theological Introduction* (Provo, Utah: Neal A. Maxwell Institute for Religious Scholarship, 2020), 74–80.

NOTES

8. David M. Goldenberg, *The Curse of Ham: Race and Slavery in Early Judaism, Christianity, and Islam* (Princeton, NJ: Princeton University Press, 2003), 178–82. See 2 Nephi 5:21 for reference to a "skin of blackness" in the Book of Mormon.
9. Gospel Topics, "Race and the Priesthood," topics.ChurchofJesusChrist.org.
10. General Church Minutes, April 25, 1847; *RDC*, 133.
11. Nelson W. Whipple, autobiography and journal, microfilm, MS 9995, 30–31, CHL; *RDC*, 133–35. For McCary and his wife Lucy Stanton's story after their excommunication at Winter Quarters, see Angela Pulley Hudson, *Real Native Genius: How an Ex-Slave and a White Mormon became Famous Indians* (Chapel Hill: University of North Carolina Press, 2015), chapters 4–6.

Chapter 9: Latter-day Saints and the Fear of Race Mixing

1. *RDC*, 106–11.
2. William I. Appleby to Brigham Young, June 2, 1847, Brigham Young Office Files, CR 1234 1, CHL.
3. Manuscript History, CR 100 102, vol. 17, March 26, 1847, 75, CHL.
4. Appleby to Young, June 2, 1847; *RDC*, 110.
5. William I. Appleby, Autobiography and Journal, MS 1401, June 16, 1847, 177, CHL; *RDC*, 110–11.
6. Peggy Pascoe, *What Comes Naturally: Miscegenation Law and the Making of Race in America* (New York: Oxford University Press, 2009), 19–22; Elise Lemire, *"Miscegenation": Making Race in America* (Philadelphia: University of Pennsylvania Press, 2002), 47, 85–86.
7. Manuscript History, MS 155, February 8, 1844, CHL.
8. General Church Minutes, CR 100 318, December 3, 1847, 6–7, CHL; *RDC*, 135.
9. General Church Minutes, December 3, 1847, 6–7; *RDC*, 135.
10. General Church Minutes, December 3, 1847, 6–7; *RDC*, 135.
11. Brigham Young, February 5, 1852, CR 100 912, CHL; Brigham Young, "The Persecutions of the Saints," March 8, 1863, *JD*, 10:110.
12. Brigham Young, March 17, 1848, CR 100 318, CHL.
13. *RDC*, 81–86, 107–11, 128–39, 145, 158–59, 180–81, 203, 253; for an example of a racial lynching in Salt Lake City tied to race mixing, see "Found Dead," *Salt Lake Daily Telegraph*, December 12, 1866, 3.
14. General Church Minutes, December 3, 1847, 6–7; *RDC*, 135–36.
15. General Church Minutes, December 3, 1847, 6–7.
16. General Church Minutes, December 3, 1847, 6–7; *RDC*, 136.
17. Josiah Clark Nott, "The Mulatto a Hybrid—Probable Extermination of the Two Races if the Whites and Blacks are Allowed to Intermarry," *American Journal of the Medical Sciences* 6 (1843): 252–56; Josiah Clark Nott, *Two Lectures on the Natural History of the Caucasian and Negro Races* (Mobile, Alabama: Dade and Thompson, 1844), 30–35; *RDC*, 136–37.
18. General Church Minutes, December 3, 1847, 6–7.

NOTES

19. Appleby, Autobiography and Journal, December 3, 1847, 203–4.
20. *RDC*, chapter 5; Brigham Young, before the Territorial Legislature, January 23, 1852, CR 100 912, CHL; Orson Pratt, before the Territorial Legislature on slavery, January 27, 1852, CR 100 912, CHL; Brigham Young, February 4, 1852, CR 100 912, CHL; Brigham Young, February 5, 1852, CR 100 912, CHL; Orson Pratt, March 22, 1856, before the 1856 Utah Constitutional Convention, MS 2988, CHL.

Chapter 10: Brigham Young Openly Articulates a Racial Restriction

1. Utah Territorial Census, 1851, Utah, Salt Lake, and Davis Counties, Schedule 2, MS 2672, 10, 23, CHL.
2. Amy Tanner Thiriot, *Slaves in Zion: African American Servitude in Utah Territory* (Salt Lake City: University of Utah Press, 2022).
3. Matthew J. Grow and Ronald W. Walker, *The Prophet and the Reformer: The Letters of Brigham Young and Thomas L. Kane* (New York: Oxford University Press, 2015), 68–69.
4. *WWJ*, November 26, 1848, 3:514.
5. W. Paul Reeve, Christopher B. Rich Jr., and LaJean Purcell Carruth, *This Abominable Slavery: Race, Religion, and the Battle over Human Bondage in Antebellum Utah* (New York: Oxford University Press), chapter 6.
6. "To the Saints," *Deseret News*, April 3, 1852, 2.
7. Orson Pratt, "The Pre-Existence of Man," *The Seer* (Washington, D.C.), April 1853; "Southern Women and Slavery," *St. Louis Luminary*, (St. Louis, MO), March 24, 1855, 70; "African Discoveries," *Western Standard*, (San Francisco, CA) February 7, 1857, 2; "Remarks on J. R. Giddings's Letter," *The Mormon* (New York), September 12, 1857, 2.
8. Church Historian's Office, General Church Minutes, CR 100 318, February 13, 1849, CHL; *RDC*, 146.
9. Jonathan Stapley, *The Power of Godliness: Mormon Liturgy and Cosmology* (New York: Oxford University Press, 2018), 20–22.
10. Church Historian's Office, General Church Minutes, February 13, 1849; *RDC*, 146.
11. Brigham Young, before the Territorial Legislature, January 23, 1852, CR 100 912, CHL; *RDC*, 149–50.
12. Orson Pratt, before the Territorial Legislature on slavery, January 27, 1852, CR 100 912, CHL.
13. Orson Pratt, January 27, 1852.
14. Orson Pratt, January 27, 1852.
15. Orson Pratt, January 27, 1852.
16. Orson Pratt, January 27, 1852.
17. Juanita Brooks, ed., *On the Mormon Frontier: The Diary of Hosea*

NOTES

Stout, 1844–1861, 2 vols. (Salt Lake City: University of Utah Press and Utah State Historical Society, 1964), 2:423.
18. Brigham Young, February 4, 1852, CR 100 912, CHL; *RDC*, 152–53.
19. Brigham Young, February 5, 1852, CR 100 912, CHL.
20. Young, February 5, 1852.
21. Young, February 5, 1852.
22. Orson Pratt, March 22, 1856, before the 1856 Utah Constitutional Convention, MS 2988, CHL.
23. Church Historian's Office, General Church Minutes, 1839–1877, CR 100 318, March 26, 1847, CHL.
24. Young, February 5, 1852.
25. Young, February 5, 1852.
26. Young, February 5, 1852.
27. Young, February 5, 1852.
28. *Journals of the House of Representatives, Council, and Joint Sessions of the First Annual and Special Sessions of the Legislative Assembly of the Territory of Utah. Held at Great Salt Lake City, 1851 and 1852* (Great Salt Lake City, Utah: Brigham H. Young, printer, 1852), 127–28.

Chapter 11: Orson Pratt and a Premortal Explanation

1. Gospel Topics, "Race and the Priesthood," topics.ChurchofJesusChrist.org.
2. Articles of Faith 1:2.
3. Orson Pratt, "The Pre-Existence of Man," *The Seer* (Washington, D.C.), April 1853.
4. Pratt, "The Pre-Existence of Man."
5. Pratt, "The Pre-Existence of Man."
6. Pratt, "The Pre-Existence of Man."
7. *Speech of Elder Orson Hyde Delivered Before the High Priests' Quorum, in Nauvoo, April 27th, 1845* (Liverpool: James and Woodburn, 1845), 30.
8. *WWJ*, December 25, 1869, 4:185.
9. B. H. Roberts, "To the Youth of Israel," *The Contributor*, May 1885, 297.
10. Joseph F. Smith Jr. to Alfred M. Nelson, January 13, 1907, MS 14591, CHL; *RDC*, 255.
11. John A. Widtsoe, "Were Negroes Neutrals in Heaven?," *Improvement Era*, June 1944, 385.
12. Joseph Fielding Smith, *Answers to Gospel Questions*, 5 vols. (Salt Lake City: Deseret Book, 1966), 5:163–64; *RDC*, 255.
13. In *The Joseph Smith Papers, Journals, Volume 2: December 1841–April 1843*, ed. Andrew H. Hedges, Alex D. Smith, and Richard Lloyd Anderson, (Salt Lake City, UT: Church Historian's Press, 2011), 212.
14. In *Council of Fifty, Minutes*, ed. Matthew J. Grow, Ronald K. Esplin, Mark Ashurst-McGee, Jeffrey D. Mahas, Matthew C. Godfrey,

NOTES

Gerrit J. Dirkmaat (Salt Lake City, UT: Church Historian's Press, September 2016), 111–13.
15. Gospel Topics, "Race and the Priesthood," topics.ChurchofJesusChrist.org.

Chapter 12: The Priesthood and Temple Restrictions in Practice

1. See W. Paul Reeve, "Elijah Able," "Mary Ann Adams Able," and "Moroni Able" at *CBM*.
2. Reeve, "Elijah Able"; Reeve, "Mary Ann Adams Able."
3. A Record of all the Quorums of Seventies in The Church of Jesus Christ of Latter-day Saints, CR 3 51, CHL.
4. W. Paul Reeve, "Moroni Able," *CBM*, https://exhibits.lib.utah.edu/s/century-of-black-mormons/page/able-moroni.
5. "Died," *Ogden Junction* (Ogden, Utah), October 25, 1871, 3; Reeve, "Moroni Able."
6. L. John Nuttall, diary, vol. 1, typescript, 290–93, BYU; *RDC*, 195–99.
7. Joseph F. Smith, Notes on Elijah Able, undated [likely ca. 1879], Joseph F. Smith Papers, CHL.
8. Council Meeting, June 4, 1879, Lester E. Bush papers, MS 685, JWML.
9. Missionary Department missionary registers, 1860–1959, 23 October 1883, Vol. 2, page 75, Line 2955, CHL.
10. "Able," *Deseret News* (Salt Lake City, Utah), December 31, 1884, 16.

Chapter 13: A One-Drop Policy

1. Tonya S. Reiter, "Rebecca Henrietta Foscue Bentley Meads," *CBM*, https://exhibits.lib.utah.edu/s/century-of-black-mormons/page/meads-rebecca-henrietta-foscue-bentley.
2. Reiter, "Rebecca Henrietta Foscue Bentley Meads."
3. Reiter, "Rebecca Henrietta Foscue Bentley Meads."
4. Reiter, "Rebecca Henrietta Foscue Bentley Meads."
5. Joseph E. Taylor to John Taylor, September 5, 1885, CHL.
6. Taylor to Taylor, September 5, 1885.
7. Daniel J. Fairbanks, *Everyone Is African: How Science Explodes the Myth of Race* (Amherst, New York: Prometheus Books, 2015), 43.
8. Fairbanks, *Everyone Is African*, 28.
9. Ariela J. Gross, *What Blood Won't Tell: A History of Race on Trial in America* (Cambridge, MA: Harvard University Press, 2008), 43–44; A. Leon Higginbotham Jr. and Barbara K. Kopytoff, "Racial Purity and Interracial Sex in the Law of Colonial and Antebellum Virginia," in *Interracialism: Black-White Intermarriage in American History, Literature, and Law*, ed. Werner Sollors (New York: Oxford University Press, 2000), 89–94; *RDC*, 192.
10. George Q. Cannon, Journal, August 18, 1900, The Journal of

NOTES

George Q. Cannon, Church Historian's Press, https://www.church historianspress.org/george-q-cannon/1900s/1900/08-1900?lang=eng.

11. Extract from George F. Richards, Record of Decisions by the Council of the First Presidency and the Twelve Apostles (no date given but the next decision in order is dated 8 February 1907), in George A. Smith Family Papers, MS 36, JWML.
12. Quincy D. Newell, *Your Sister in the Gospel: The Life of Jane Manning James, A Nineteenth-Century Black Mormon* (New York: Oxford University Press, 2019), chapter 7.
13. Jane E. James to John Taylor, December 27, 1884, CHL.
14. James to Taylor, December 27, 1884; Jane E. James to Joseph F. Smith, February 7, 1890, CHL; *RDC*, 200–203.
15. Adoption Record, Book A, 26, CHL; *RDC*, 202.
16. "Funeral of Isaac Manning," *Deseret Evening News*, April 17, 1911, 3.
17. "Prophet's Servant, Old Negro, dead," *Salt Lake Telegram*, April 13, 1911, 12.
18. "Roberts, Young, Wells and Kimball Speakers at Mormon Conference," *Salt Lake Telegram*, April 7, 1906, 2.
19. W. Paul Reeve, "'I Dug the Graves': Isaac Lewis Manning, Joseph Smith, and Racial Connections in Two Latter-day Saint Traditions," *Journal of Mormon History* 47 (January 2021): 59–67.

Chapter 14: The Restrictions Harden in Place

1. George A. Smith Family Papers, MS 36, Council Meeting, August 26, 1908, JWML; *RDC*, 208–10.
2. George A. Smith Family Papers, Council Minutes, August 22, 1895; David McKay, to John R. Winder, March 14, 1904, Joseph F. Smith, Stake Correspondence, CR 1 191, CHL.
3. George A. Smith Family Papers, Council Minutes, August 26, 1908.
4. George A. Smith Family Papers, Council Minutes, August 26, 1908.
5. "From Far-off Africa," *Liahona*, August 1, 1908, 151.
6. German E. Ellsworth, Letter to Joseph F. Smith, December 24, 1909, Northern States Mission, CHL; *RDC*, 253.
7. Marie Graves, to Heber J. Grant, November 10, 1920, CHL.
8. Historian Ardis E. Parshall uncovered William and Marie's stories, the details of which can be found at Ardis E. Parshall, "William and Marie Graves: 'We found the right church all right,'" September 30, 2015, *Keepapitchinin*, http://www.keepapitchinin.org/2018/09/12/william-and-marie-graves-we-found-the-right-church-all-right/; Ardis E. Parshall, "William and Marie Graves: The Part I Withheld," September 14, 2018, *Keepapitchinin*, http://www.keepapitchinin.org/2018/09/14/marie-and-william-graves-the-part-i-withheld/.
9. Heber J. Grant to Joseph W. McMurrin, November 23, 1920, CHL; Parshall, "The Part I Withheld."

NOTES

Chapter 15: A Lack of Consensus for Change

1. "LDS Church First Presidency Statement," August 17, 1949, CHL, in Matthew L. Harris and Newell G. Bringhurst, *The Mormon Church and Blacks: A Documentary History* (Urbana: University of Illinois Press, 2015), 64–66.
2. Mark E. Petersen, "Race Problems—As They Affect the Church" (address to Church Educational System religious educators, August 27, 1954), CHL.
3. Bruce R. McConkie, *Mormon Doctrine* (Salt Lake City: Bookcraft, 1958), 102.
4. McConkie, *Mormon Doctrine*, 108; emphasis in the original.
5. McConkie, *Mormon Doctrine*, 476–77.
6. Harvard S. Heath, ed., *Confidence amid Change: The Presidential Diaries of David O. McKay, 1951–1970* (Salt Lake City: Signature Books, 2019), 300–304.
7. Bruce R. McConkie, *Mormon Doctrine* (Salt Lake City: Bookcraft, 1979), 114; Harris and Bringhurst, *The Mormon Church and Blacks*, 71–72.
8. First Presidency statement of December 15, 1969, "Church Section," *Deseret News*, January 10, 1970, 12; *RDC*, 256.
9. Roger S. Porter, "Educator Cites McKay Statement of No Negro Bias in LDS Tenets," *Salt Lake Tribune,* January 15, 1970, 33.
10. Edward L. Kimball, "Spencer W. Kimball and the Revelation on Priesthood," *BYU Studies* 47, no. 2 (2008): 21–22, 27.
11. Newell G. Bringhurst, *Harold B. Lee: Life and Thought* (Salt Lake City: Signature Books, 2021), 98–105.
12. Hugh B. Brown, in Conference Report (Salt Lake City: The Church of Jesus Christ of Latter-day Saints, 1963), 91.
13. Ezra Taft Benson, in Conference Report (Salt Lake City: The Church of Jesus Christ of Latter-day Saints, 1967), 34–38.
14. Edward L. Kimball, ed., *The Teachings of Spencer W. Kimball: Twelfth President of the Church of Jesus Christ of Latter-day Saints* (Salt Lake City: Bookcraft, 1982), 448–49.

Chapter 16: Racial Restrictions and the International Church

1. Heber C. Meeks, Report to the First Presidency, July 23, 1947, in Russell W. Stevenson, *For the Cause of Righteousness: A Global History of Blacks and Mormonism, 1830–2013* (Salt Lake City: Greg Kofford Books, 2014), 305–6.
2. Heber C. Meeks to Lowery Nelson, June 20, 1947, in Stevenson, *For the Cause of Righteousness*, 304.
3. Meeks, Report to the First Presidency.
4. George Albert Smith, J. Reuben Clark Jr., and David O. McKay, to Francis W. Brown, January 13, 1947, Lester E. Bush papers, MS 685, JWML; *RDC*, 254.
5. Matthew L. Harris and Newell G. Bringhurst, *The Mormon Church*

and Blacks: A Documentary History (Urbana: University of Illinois Press, 2015), 101–3; Jeremy Talmage and Clinton D. Christensen, "Black, White, or Brown? Racial Perceptions and the Priesthood Policy in Latin America," *Journal of Mormon History* 44 (January 2018): 132–41.
6. "Lineage Lesson," Brazil North Mission, 1970, in Harris and Bringhurst, *The Mormon Church and Blacks*, 103–5.
7. Talmage and Christensen, "Black, White, or Brown?," 119–45.
8. Talmage and Christensen, "Black, White, or Brown?," 124–25.
9. Talmage and Christensen, "Black, White, or Brown?," 124–25.
10. Talmage and Christensen, "Black, White, or Brown?," 125–26.
11. Talmage and Christensen, "Black, White, or Brown?," 126.
12. Talmage and Christensen, "Black, White, or Brown?," 125–29.
13. Talmage and Christensen, "Black, White, or Brown?," 131–32.
14. Talmage and Christensen, "Black, White, or Brown?," 132.
15. Talmage and Christensen, "Black, White, or Brown?," 132–41.
16. Talmage and Christensen, "Black, White, or Brown?," 140–41.
17. Talmage and Christensen, "Black, White, or Brown?," 141–43.
18. Talmage and Christensen, "Black, White, or Brown?," 142–43.
19. Joseph Johnson, "History of the Church of Jesus Christ of Latter-day Saints in Ghana," in Stevenson, *For the Cause of Righteousness,* 326–27.
20. Stevenson, *For the Cause of Righteousness*, 188–97; James B. Allen, "Would-Be Saints: West Africa before the 1978 Priesthood Revelation," *Journal of Mormon History* 17 (Winter 1991): 205–47; Edward L. Kimball, "Spencer W. Kimball and the Revelation on Priesthood," *BYU Studies* 47, no. 2 (2008): 23.
21. Mark L. Grover, "Religious Accommodation in the Land of Racial Democracy: Mormon Priesthood and Black Brazilians," *Dialogue: A Journal of Mormon Thought* 17 (Autumn 1984): 23–34; Mark L. Grover, "The Mormon Priesthood Revelation and the São Paulo, Brazil Temple," *Dialogue: A Journal of Mormon Thought* 23 (Spring 1990): 39–53.
22. LeGrand Richards interview with Wesley P. Walters and Chris Vlachos, August 16, 1978, in Harris and Bringhurst, *The Mormon Church and Blacks*, 114.

Chapter 17: The 1978 Revelation

1. W. Paul Reeve, "Freda Lucretia Magee Beaulieu," *CBM*, https://exhibits.lib.utah.edu/s/century-of-black-mormons/page/beaulieu-freda-lucretia-magee.
2. Reeve, "Freda Lucretia Magee Beaulieu."
3. Spencer W. Kimball to Edward Kimball, March 11, 1963, in Edward L. Kimball, "Spencer W. Kimball and the Revelation on Priesthood," *BYU Studies* 47, no. 2 (2008): 46.
4. Kimball, "Revelation on Priesthood," 48.
5. Kimball, "Revelation on Priesthood," 50.

6. Kimball, "Revelation on Priesthood," 64.
7. Kimball, "Revelation on Priesthood," 45.
8. Kimball, "Revelation on Priesthood," 54.
9. Kimball, "Revelation on Priesthood," 27.
10. Kimball, "Revelation on Priesthood," 10, 19.
11. Kimball, "Revelation on Priesthood," 44–54.
12. Kimball, "Revelation on Priesthood," 52.
13. Kimball, "Revelation on Priesthood," 56.
14. Kimball, "Revelation on Priesthood," 56–57.
15. "Report from the Presidency," *Times and Seasons* (Nauvoo, Illinois), October 1840, 188.
16. Reeve, "Freda Lucretia Magee Beaulieu."
17. Freda Lucretia Magee Beaulieu, address, January 16, 1982, MS 6938, 5, CHL.
18. Beaulieu, address; Reeve, "Freda Lucretia Magee Beaulieu."
19. Beaulieu, address; Reeve, "Freda Lucretia Magee Beaulieu."
20. Beaulieu, address; Reeve, "Freda Lucretia Magee Beaulieu."
21. Robert B. Evans to James Kimball, February 20, 1982, MS 6983, CHL; Parker P. Warner, "South Louisiana District," *Liahona: The Elders' Journal* (Independence, MO) vol. 42, no. 12 (November 28, 1944), 286; Reeve, "Freda Lucretia Magee Beaulieu."
22. Warner, "South Louisiana District"; Reeve, "Freda Lucretia Magee Beaulieu."
23. Evans to Kimball, February 20, 1982; Warner, "South Louisiana District."
24. Warner, "South Louisiana District."
25. Warner, "South Louisiana District"; Reeve, "Freda Lucretia Magee Beaulieu."
26. Reeve, "Freda Lucretia Magee Beaulieu."

Chapter 18: Post-Revelation Justifications

1. Bruce R. McConkie, "All Are Alike unto God" (address given at the Church Educational System Symposium, August 17–19, 1978).
2. Dieter F. Uchtdorf, "Acting on the Truths of the Gospel of Jesus Christ" (worldwide leadership training meeting, February 2012), https://www.ChurchofJesusChrist.org/broadcasts/article/worldwide-leadership-training/2012/01/acting-on-the-truths-of-the-gospel-of-jesus-christ?lang=eng.
3. Dallin H. Oaks, "Love Your Enemies," *Ensign*, November 2020.
4. Daniel J. Fairbanks, *Everyone Is African: How Science Explodes the Myth of Race* (Amhurst, New York: Prometheus Books, 2015), 43.
5. Fairbanks, *Everyone Is African*, 43.
6. Fairbanks, *Everyone Is African*, 23, 33.
7. Fairbanks, *Everyone Is African*, 62–63.
8. J. Reuben Clark Jr., *On the Way to Immortality and Eternal Life* (Salt Lake City: Deseret Book, 1949), 154.
9. Ardis Parshall, "A Stealthy Return to Bad Practice of the Past," http://

www.keepapitchinin.org/2016/07/05/draft-a-stealthy-return-to-bad-practices-of-the-past/.
10. "Church History," *Times and Seasons* (Nauvoo, Illinois), March 1, 1842, 709.
11. Manumission records, quoted in Allan Kulikoff, *Tobacco and Slaves: The Development of Southern Cultures in the Chesapeake, 1680–1800* (Chapel Hill: University of North Carolina Press, 1986), 432–33.
12. Sidney Rigdon, "To the Honorable, the Senate and House of Representatives of Pennsylvania, in Legislative Capacity Assembled," *Times and Seasons* (Nauvoo, Illinois), February 1, 1844, 422.

Chapter 19: Agency and the Gospel Plan

1. Orson Pratt, March 22, 1856, before the 1856 Utah Constitutional Convention, transcribed from John V. Long's shorthand record by LaJean Purcell Carruth, Utah Territory Constitutional Convention Papers, 1856, MS 2988, CHL.

    Portions of this chapter are drawn from W. Paul Reeve, "I am a Believer, but I Don't 'Just Believe,'" https://www.fairlatterdaysaints.org/testimonies/scholars/w-paul-reeve.
2. Ezra Taft Benson, "Jesus Christ—Gifts and Expectations," *New Era*, May 1975, 16.
3. Russell M. Nelson, "The Power of Spiritual Momentum," *Liahona*, May 2022.
4. Dieter F. Uchtdorf, "Come, Join with Us," *Ensign*, November 2013.
5. Jeffrey R. Holland, "Lord, I Believe," *Ensign*, May 2013.

Chapter 20: Prophetic Leadership

1. Official Declaration 1.
2. *The Late Corporation of the Church of Jesus Christ of Latter-day Saints v. United States*, 136, U.S. 1 (1890).
3. Official Declaration 1.

Chapter 21: Jesus Christ Is Mighty to Save

1. Spencer W. Kimball, "Our Own Liahona," *Ensign*, November 1976.
2. Joseph F. Smith to A. Saxey, January 7, 1897, CHL.
3. Terryl Givens and Fiona Givens, *The Crucible of Doubt: Reflections on the Quest for Faith* (Salt Lake City: Deseret Book, 2014), 70.
4. On eternal progression, see Gospel Topics, "Becoming Like God," topics.ChurchofJesusChrist.org.
5. "Church Statement Regarding 'Washington Post' Article on Race and the Church," https://newsroom.ChurchofJesusChrist.org/article/racial-remarks-in-washington-post-article.
6. R. Scott Lloyd, "FamilySearch Announces Project to Index 4 Million Records of Freed Slaves," June 19, 2015, https://www.ChurchofJesusChrist.org/church/news/familysearch-announces-project-to-index-4-million-records-of-freed-slaves?lang=eng.
7. "Church Donates $2 Million to the International African American

NOTES

Museum," February 27, 2019, https://newsroom.ChurchofJesusChrist.org/article/church-donation-2-million-international-african-american-museum-center-family-history.
8. "Locking arms for Racial Harmony in America: What the NAACP and The Church of Jesus Christ of Latter-day Saints are doing together," June 8, 2020, https://medium.com/@Ch_JesusChrist/locking-arms-for-racial-harmony-in-america-2f62180abf37.
9. Gordon B. Hinckley, "The Need for Greater Kindness," *Ensign*, May 2006.
10. M. Russell Ballard, "The Trek Continues!" *Ensign*, November 2017.
11. Dallin H. Oaks, "Racism and Other Challenges" (Brigham Young University devotional, October 27, 2020), https://speeches.byu.edu/talks/dallin-h-oaks/racism-other-challenges/.
12. Russell M. Nelson, "Let God Prevail," *Ensign*, November 2020.

Chapter 22: A Path Forward

1. Russell M. Nelson, "Let God Prevail," *Ensign*, November 2020.
2. Dallin H. Oaks, "Love Your Enemies," *Ensign*, November 2020.
3. W. Paul Reeve, "Making Sense of the Church's History on Race," June 30, 2020, *Faith Matters*, https://faithmatters.org/making-sense-of-the-churchs-history-on-race/.
4. [William G. Hartley], "Saint Without Priesthood," *Dialogue: A Journal of Mormon Thought* 12, no. 2 (Summer 1979): 18.

INDEX

Able, Elijah, 12–13, 75–78, 85, 107, 132
Able, Mary Ann Adams, 12, 75
Able, Moroni, 75, 76
Abolitionism, 24, 27–28, 34–38. *See also* emancipation
Abraham, book of, 47–53
Act for the Relief of Indian Slaves and Prisoners, An, 62, 63
Act in Relation to Service, An, 62–63, 64–66
Adam-God theory, 127
Adams, Mary Ann, 12, 75
Africa, 98–99
Agency, 5, 71, 120–24
Allen, Charles, 30
American Colonization Society, 27
Appleby, William I., 57–58, 59–60

Badger, Ralph A., 85
Ballard, M. Russell, 129
Baptism, of enslaved people, 19–20
Bartholow, Roberts, 32–33
Beaulieu, Freda Lucretia Magee, 103, 106–9, 132
Beaulieu, Rudolph, 108
Benson, Ezra Taft, 91, 121
Berry, Laura, 80
Betsy (enslaved girl), 20–21
Black converts, 11–23
Brazil, 93–94, 96–97, 99
Brown, Elizabeth Crosby, 20
Brown, Hugh B., 91
Brown, John, 20
Brown v. Board of Education (1954), 88–89
Bullock, Thomas, 61
Burton, John, 18–19
Burton, Susan McCord, 18, 19
Bush, Lester E., 104–5

Cain, curse of, 50–51, 64, 66–67, 68, 70, 72, 73, 89–90, 127. *See also* curses, Old Testament
Calhoun, John C., 26
Canaan, curse of, 35–36, 47–53. *See also* curses, Old Testament
Cannon, George Q., 82
Caste system, 89–90
Chambers, Amanda, 21
Chambers, Samuel, 21–23, 133
Church of Jesus Christ of Latter-day Saints, The: bearing burden of and learning from past of, 5–6, 131; phases of racial priesthood and temple restrictions in, 7; Black converts to, 11–23; persecution against, 29–30, 31, 34; outsiders' racial view of, 31–33; and slavery in 1830s and '40s, 34–40; division in, following martyrdom, 47; survey of eastern branches, 57–58; policy regarding slavery, 62; racial restrictions and international, 93–99; ordination of Black men as possibly detrimental to, 116–17; racism condemned by, 128, 129–30, 131. *See also* gospel; missionary work
Civil rights, 89, 90, 91
Clark, J. Reuben, 115
Cobos, Benigno, 94–95
Colombia, 97–98
Constitution, 39
Contieri, Eduardo, 96
Copland, Charles, 118
Cuba, 93
Cuesta, Guillermo, 96
Curses, Old Testament, 35–36, 47–53, 64, 65, 66–67, 68,

INDEX

70–71, 72, 73, 89–90, 113–14, 127

Dana, Lewis, 41
Darkness, 51–52
Deacons, 21–22
"Declaration of Belief Regarding Governments and Laws in General," 34–35
De la Cruz, María, 94
DNA, 80–81, 114
Douglass, Frederick, 19

Ecuador, 96
Emancipation, 25, 27–28, 34, 37–38. *See also* abolitionism
Enslaved people: as converts, 18–22; as pioneers, 18–22, 62; and colonization of Africa, 27; in Utah Territory, 62–63; in Latin America, 93–94; freeing of, 118; family history records of, 128–29. *See also* abolitionism; emancipation; slavery
Equality, 2, 7, 25, 26–27, 37, 39, 68–69, 74, 118–19, 131–33
Eternal progression, 128
Evans, Robert B., 108, 109

Fairbanks, Daniel J., 81
Family history work, 128–29
Foscue, Lewis, 79
Foscue, Rebecca Henrietta, 79–80
Freedmen's Bank and Bureau records, 128
"Free People of Color" (Phelps), 24, 27–30

Gadsden's Wharf, 129
Garrison, William Lloyd, 27
Genetics, 80–81, 114
Ghana, 98
Givens, Terryl and Fiona, 128
God: racism as source of weeping of, 6; attributes of, 112–13, 132
Gont, Mary, 41
Gospel: as inclusive, 11–12, 16–17, 24, 28–29, 38–39; spreading of, 115, 117; agency in, 120–24. *See also* Church of Jesus Christ of Latter-day Saints, The; missionary work
Grant, Heber J., 87
Graves, Marie, 86–87, 132
Graves, William, 86–87

Haight, David B., 106
Ham, curse of, 35–36, 47–53
Hinckley, Gordon B., 106, 129
History, learning from, 131
Hofheintz, Peter, 42
Holland, Jeffrey R., 122
Honduras, 95–96
Howells, Rulon S., 94
Hunter, Howard W., 97
Hyde, Orson, 59, 60, 72

Imperfection, 121–24, 128
Indian Removal Act, 24
Insignares, Horacio, 97–98
International African American Museum, 129
Interracial marriage, 25, 27, 37, 41, 44–45, 57–61, 67–68, 74, 93–94

Jackson County, Missouri, 24–30, 34
James, Jane Elizabeth Manning, 14–15, 16, 79, 82–84, 132
Jefferson, Thomas, 118
Jesus Christ: ministry of, 115; and fallibility of prophets, 123–24; attributes of, 132
Johnson, Joseph, 98

Kane, Thomas L., 62
Kemp, Donald Richard, 4
Kimball, Edward, 104, 105
Kimball, Heber C., 32, 59
Kimball, Spencer W., 91–92, 96, 98, 99, 103–6
Kinney, Eunice, 13
Koepsel, Ernest, 103

INDEX

Lamanites, 51, 52
Latin America, 93–98, 99
Lee, Harold B., 91
Levi, tribe of, 116
Lewis, Enoch, 57–58, 59, 67–68
Lewis, Q. Walker, 13–14, 45, 46, 57–58, 59, 67, 118
Light and dark metaphors, 51–52

Magee, Ardella, 103, 107
Magee, Flanders, 103
Magee, Freda Lucretia, 103, 106–9, 132
Magee, Percy, 103
Magee, Samuel, 103, 107
Magee, Vander, 103
Manifesto (1890), 125–26
Mann, William C., 1
Manning, Isaac, 15, 16, 83–84
Manning, Jane Elizabeth, 14–15, 16, 79, 82–84, 132
Manning, Sarah, 16
May, Robert H. Jr., 107–8
McCary, William, 44–46, 47, 52–53, 67–68
McConkie, Bruce R., 89–90, 106, 110
McKay, David O., 90, 91, 105
McMurrin, Sterling M., 91
Meads, Nathan, 79–80
Meeks, Heber C., 93
Mexico, 94–95
Missionary work: revelations concerning, 11–12; of Elijah Able, 13; among Black people, 14–15, 18, 22, 40, 85–87; hopes for, in Nauvoo, 41; and slavery in Utah Territory, 65; in Latin America, 93–94; and spreading gospel, 115, 117
Mob violence, in Missouri, 29–30, 31, 34
Mode, Jesse, 42
Mode, Sarah Ann, 42–43
Mortality, 64, 120, 121, 122

National Association for the Advancement of Colored People (NAACP), 129
Native Americans, 41. *See also* McCary, William
Nauvoo, Illinois, 41–43
Nelson, Russell M., 2, 121, 129, 130, 131
Nephites, 52
New information, accepting, 111–12
Nigeria, 98–99
Noah, curse of, 35–36, 47–53. *See also* Old Testament curses
Nott, Josiah Clark, 61

Oaks, Dallin H., 113, 130
Ocampo, Roberto, 95–96
Old Testament curses, 35–36, 47–53, 64, 65, 66–67, 68, 70–71, 72, 73, 89–90, 113–14, 127
Olson, Kirt, 97–98
One-drop policy, 79–84
Opposition, 122
Original sin, 36, 70
Ourselves, esteeming others as, 131–33

Page, John E., 13
Parshall, Ardis, 116
Partridge, Edward, 30
Patriarch and patriarchal descent, 48
Perry, L. Tom, 106
Persecution, in Missouri, 29–30, 31, 34
Peter (Black convert), 11
Peter (disciple), 115
Petersen, Mark E., 88–89, 90
Pharaoh, 48
Phelps, William Wines, 24, 27–30
Pioneers, enslaved people as, 18–22, 62
Plan of salvation, 120–24
Plessy v. Fergusson (1896), 81

INDEX

Plural marriage, 32–33, 117, 125–26

Politics, race and, 26

Polygamy, 32–33, 117, 125–26

Pratt, Orson, 61, 63, 64–66, 67, 69, 70–74, 118, 120–21

Pratt, Parley P., 31, 47, 49, 52

Premortal life, 64, 70–74, 113

Presentism, 117–19

Priesthood: Black men's ordinations to, in early church, 12–14; history of ordinations to, 14; tribe of Levi and, 116. *See also* priesthood restriction

Priesthood restriction: phases of, 7; openly espoused by Brigham Young, 62–69; premortal explanation for, 70–74; in practice, 75–78; and one-drop policy, 79–84; hardening of, 85–87; lack of consensus regarding, 88–92; and international Church, 93–99; revelation reversing, 103–6; origins of, 105, 110–11, 114, 127; scriptural basis for, 105; justifications for, 110–19; agency and, 120–24; impact of, 127–28

Prophets: fallibility of, 120–24, 128; trusting, 125–26

Race: challenges of defining, 5; and inclusive gospel, 11–12, 16–17, 24, 38–39; in Jackson County, Missouri, 24–30; nineteenth-century views on, 25–27; and outsiders' view of Church, 31–33; and Old Testament curses, 35–36, 47–53, 64, 65, 66–67, 68, 70–71, 72, 73, 89–90, 113–14; Joseph Smith on, 37, 74; one-drop policy, 79–84; segregation based on, 81, 88–89, 110–11; caste system based on, 89–90. *See also* priesthood restriction; race mixing; racial equality; racism; temple restriction

Race mixing, 25, 27, 37, 41, 44–45, 57–61, 67–68, 74, 93–94

Racial equality, 2, 7, 25, 26–27, 37, 39, 68–69, 74, 118–19, 131–33

Racism: bearing burden of Church's past, 5–6; as source of God's weeping, 6; against Black church members, 86–87; against Latin American church members, 94–98; taught to Spencer W. Kimball, 104; as multigenerational, 113; rooting out, 113–14, 129–30, 131; and impact of ordination of Black men on church, 116–17; in past, 117–19; as condemned by Church, 128, 129–30, 131; repenting of, 129

Repentance, 50, 51, 121, 129

Revelation(s): regarding inclusive gospel, 11–12; reversing priesthood and temple restrictions, 103–6, 110; accepting, 111–12

Richards, LeGrand, 99

Richards, Willard, 59, 63

Rigdon, Sidney, 118

Ritchie, Nelson Holder, 1–3

Ritchie, Russell Dewey, 3–4

Roberts, Brigham H., 73

Roberts, Ezekiel, 12

Robinson, Joseph Lee, 18, 19

Romney, Marion G., 90, 104

Russell, Annie Cowan, 1, 2, 3

Salvation, 127–28. *See also* plan of salvation

Samaritans, 115

São Paulo Brazil Temple, 99

Sealings, 1–3, 4, 41, 42, 64, 75, 79, 80

Second Article of Faith, 36, 70

Segregation, 81, 88–89, 110–11

Slavery, 19, 22, 25, 26, 34–40,

INDEX

62–66. *See also* abolitionism; emancipation; enslaved people
Smith, Emma, 15–16, 83
Smith, George A., 64
Smith, Hyrum, 16, 48
Smith, Joseph F., 77, 82, 84, 85, 127
Smith, Joseph Fielding, 73–74
Smith, Joseph Jr.: models inclusive society, 15–17; on slavery, 34, 35–39; on race, 37, 74; church leadership following martyrdom of, 47–48; and interracial marriage, 58–59; on original sin, 70; on priesthood and eternal life, 75–76; Jane Manning "attached" by proxy to, 83; on spread of gospel, 117; as product of nineteenth century, 118; fallibility of, 121–22
Smith, Joseph Sr., 48
Smith, Milton E., 95
Snow, Lorenzo, 63–64, 82, 110
Stanton, Lucy, 44–45
Stebbins family, 15–16
Stout, Hosea, 66
Strange, James, 47
Supreme Court, 33, 125–26

Tanner, N. Eldon, 106
Taylor, John, 76–77, 83
Taylor, Joseph E., 80
Temple blessings: received by Black members in early church, 12–13, 42–43; and interracial marriage, 68
Temple restriction: experienced by Nelson Holder Ritchie, 1–3; phases of, 7; in practice, 75–78; and one-drop policy, 79–84; hardening of, 85–87; lack of consensus regarding, 88–92; and international Church, 93–99; revelation reversing, 103–6; origins of, 105, 110–11, 114; justifications for, 110–19; agency and, 120–24; impact of, 127–28

Uchtdorf, Dieter F., 111–12, 122
Universalism, 41–43
U.S. Constitution, 39

Voting rights, 63, 66, 68–69, 118

Waite, Morrison, 33
Wandell, Charles Wesley, 14
Warner, Parker P., 108–9
Webster, Mary Matilda, 57–58, 59
Westward migration, 18–22, 62
Whipple, Nelson, 52–53
Whitaker, John M., 1, 4
Widtsoe, John A., 73
Winter Quarters, 18–19, 42, 44–46, 47
Woodruff, Wilford, 14, 44, 125–26

Young, Brigham: interracial sealing performed by, 41; early opinions of, on race, 44–46; and origins of priesthood restriction, 49, 105, 110, 127; and survey of eastern branches, 57–58, 59; on race mixing, 59–61; on priesthood restriction, 62–69, 70; on acts regarding slaves and servants, 63; on premortal existence, 72; John Taylor reinforces position of, 77; as product of nineteenth century, 118; agency of, 120–21; and eternal progression, 128

Zion, 16–17, 112